ENDORSEMENTS

If You're searching for your true identity and purpose in life, look no further. Drop everything. Then read this book—*Who Says So?* Jeff Byrd offers a valuable, practical guide that will help you really understand who you are and, more importantly, whose you are. You will want to buy several copies—one for yourself and some to give to those you love.

—*Gloria J. Burgess, Author*
Flawless Leadership and Pass It On!

"This is a God-given message for the world! Your insights about abuse and self-worth alone will be revolutionary for people trying to heal from their past."

—*Ashley Welch*
Trilogy Christian Publishing, Inc.
A Wholly Owned Subsidiary of TBN

This book is a very helpful resource to living out the Christian Life. Understanding our identity that we have in Christ is essential for finding victory. Jesus said that he came to give life and life abundantly, Jeff (Mr. Byrd) highlights the work of Jesus on our behalf and the new life that is offered despite the hardships and challenges we face on this side of heaven. He delicately addresses personal brokenness, while highlighting the hope and healing that is offered to us in Jesus.

This book provides a pathway to hope, freedom and victory. It helps to address real pain and brokenness, and leads people past a victim-hood mentality to a mindset of victory. For anyone who has experienced deep hurt and pain, or struggles to believe who God says that you are, this book will help you find a better way to live.

—Pastor Kevin Tremper
CrossRoads Church
Kevin@CRCNorfolk.com

It is hard for me to write a short quote, or endorsement, of this book. The best way I do it is just say *"Read-it"*, you will not have wasted your time, but you will have enriched your life and as a consequence you will be able to enrich others.

I would recommend this book to anyone, of any age, to refresh your life. There are messages in it which everyone needs to hear, or to be reminded of. This is not a book of pure optimism but based on pure reality—the reality of purpose, the reality of life, and the reality of God!

I believe that everyone will identify with something,

and likely more than one-thing, within these pages. This is a liberating book and it will help you to find freedom. This book should be read at least once a year as a reminder of who we are and what we can do!

—Italo Gill
Pastor

If you are looking for the answer to tell you what God is trying to tell us in the Bible, "Who Says So?" is for you! Too many theologians have used too many words in way too many books—trying to explain God's purpose—Jeff does it so well here with a lot less words. Jeff's insight into God's plan for us, and our part in that plan, is simple and inspiring--it should give us all hope.

—Reverend Shaun Smith
JRD Construction Consultant
Pastor, Ft Grove, Independence, and Mt Pleasant UMC's

A truly wonderful book: intelligent, essential, and deeply insightful. After I read it, I have been recommending to everyone because it is incredibly relevant to how so many of us are probably feeling.

—Christie Fleck Privette
Founder & CEO of Two 17 Marketing

This is a brilliant and insightful combination of faith and self-enlightenment as we explore our journey to fulfill our God given purpose. Jeff is masterful in his ability to connect with people and get to the core of the issue with tenderness, laughter when needed, enthusiasm, and much needed hope in a world that seems to have been turned upside down. As you read, the book just keep getting better and better. This book can only have been written by a man who has experienced that many nuances of life and turned many negative experiences into a positive with faith, hope, and love. He weaves his life voyage and observations into this must-read book for anyone on a journey to discover who they are and who they want to be. I highly recommend this book for yourself, anyone you love, or someone at a crossroads in life. You will not be sorry for the time invested in the read and yourself.

—***Donna L Wilson, Esq.***
Founder of Wilson Law, PLC

WHO SAYS SO?

WHO SAYS SO?

UNDERSTANDING THE MESSAGES THAT SHAPE OUR HEARTS

Jeffrey W. Byrd
Author

Angela M. Byrd
Illustrator

Norfolk • Virginia • USA

Who Says So?
Understanding the Messages that Shape Our Hearts

Published by:

New Dominion Press

New Dominion Media/New Dominion Press
1217 Godfrey Avenue, Norfolk, Virginia 23504-3218
www.NewDominionPress.com

First Printing: November 2019

No part of this book may be reproduced, stored in any information storage or retrieval system, electronic or mechanical, including photocopying, recording or transmission in any form whatsoever, except in the case of short quotations printed in articles or reviews, with attribution and without the written consent of the author, except as provided by the copyright law of the United States of America.

Cover, Graphic Design, and Typography by New Dominion Press
Cover Art and Illustrations by Angela Byrd
Copy editing by Ashley Carlson

Copyright © 2019 by Jeffrey W. Byrd
All Rights Reserved

Publisher's Cataloging-in-Publication Data
provided by Five Rainbows Cataloging Services

Names: Byrd, Jeffrey W., 1967- author. | Byrd, Angela M., illustrator.
Title: Who says so? : understanding the messages that shape our hearts / Jeffrey W. Byrd ; Angela M. Byrd, illustrator.
Description: Norfolk, VA : New Dominion Press, 2019.
Identifiers: LCCN:2019905848 | ISBN 978-1-7331292-0-6 (paperback).
Subjects: LCSH: Christian life. | Identity (Psychology)--Religious aspects--Christianity. | Self-actualization (Psychology)--Religious aspects--Christianity. | Self-perception--Religious aspects--Christianity. | Self-evaluation. | Restoration movement (Christianity) | Love--Religious aspects--Christianity. | BISAC: : RELIGION / Christian Living / Personal Growth. | SELF-HELP / Personal Growth / General. | BODY, MIND & SPIRIT / Inspiration & Personal Growth.
Classification: LCC BV4501.3.B973 2019 (print) | DDC 974.7/25--dc23.

First Edition

> "The essence of all abuse lies in being devalued. The essence of all healing lies in having your value restored."
>
> —Jeffrey W. Byrd

Dedication

This book is dedicated to my beautiful wife, Angela Byrd, who has supported me so faithfully in all my undertakings.

It is also dedicated to all who suffer so much from the lies about their identity, value, and worth, that have been handed down to them by the actions and words of others.

> *May this book help to set you free—*
> *To become all you were created to be!*
>
> *—Jeffrey W. Byrd*

TABLE OF CONTENTS

Acknowledgments xvii

Foreword xxi
Barbara Valentine Gustavson

Introduction: 1
From the Beginning

Chapter One: 5
From the Beginning–The Beautiful You

Chapter Two: 17
An Intense Hatred–The War Against Us

Chapter Three: 27
Heart Messages, Family, and Abuse

Chapter Four: 45
Heart Messages and Social Interaction

Chapter Five: 59
Heart Issues and Career

Chapter Six: 73
    Heart Issues and Relationships–The Devaluing of
    Women and the Lostness of Men

Chapter Seven: 85
    Heart Issues and Religion

Chapter Eight: 107
    Now and Forever—The Restoration of All Things

Afterward: 119

Appendix 1: 121
    Who I Am—In Christ!
        (Originally compiled by Neil Anderson)

Appendix 2: 131
    A Note On Forgiveness

References: 133
    Accumulated Endnotes

Biography: 139

Book Sponsors 143
    Wilson Law, PLC
    Jeffrey Byrd Coaching
    Angela Byrd Designs
    New Dominion Press

Acknowledgments

There is no way this project could ever have come to fruition without the energy, advice, proofing, editing, and encouragement of so many whom I am grateful to know, and admire so very deeply. Over the years, there have been so many who helped me see the gifts I have and the ways I can use them to add value to others.

There are many on my list who have had a positive influence on my life, and I'm afraid I won't remember everyone who has contributed. However, a number of those who have made a lasting difference come to mind: Chap Percival, my high school physics teacher who introduced me to birding in 8th grade. As a result, I began to travel, started a photography business, and eventually met my wife through the love of birds!

Kaye Crenshaw was one of the first to truly see potential in me and was willing to give me the opportunity to use it by hiring me! Though it has been years since we worked together, she and her husband Lee, are lifelong friends, and whenever I think of those who have helped me grow, she immediately comes warmly to mind.

Christie Fleck-Privette has been one of my closest friends for many years now. She has believed in me, and my vision, from early on and is always someone whom I ask for feedback anytime I start a new project.

My friend from kindergarten, Barbara Gustavson, is the first who caused me to understand my role as a leader and who introduced me to the John Maxwell Team, where I have learned so much and gained exponential growth both personally and in my ability to help others.

Willie Butler and Chuck Christie welcomed me into their Wednesday morning prayer group several years ago and have been a strong encouragement, pushing me to pursue my calling and use my gifts to lift others. They have also provided practical needs for advice, technology, and financial guidance. Chuck's company is also the publisher of this book!

My dad, many years deceased now, remains my greatest model of a life transformed by grace and value. Though we didn't get along so well at times, he is now my greatest mentor on what it means to come to the end of oneself and come to the beginning of "God room", where He takes over and does for us what we cannot, as we humbly look to Him in faith.

My mom has always been a huge believer in me and has supported me in any way she has been able over all these years. I am truly thankful to her.

And last, but most definitely not least, is my wife Angela, who, as her name implies, is an angel, especially to me. She resolutely believes in my vision of the value of all people, my efforts to enhance the vision and skills of others in living a value-based life, and most importantly, she still believes in me and patiently supports and loves me, even when I do not live out the very things I would share with others. She stands by me in the growth process, believing not only in who I am but in who I am becoming.

From the bottom of my heart, thank you all. Your love, support, and companionship on the journey are worth more than gold!

Foreword

Barbara Valentine Gustavson

Many people quietly grapple with a continual voice in their head that questions their value, identity and purpose in life. We desire to believe that we matter and that what we do matters. Even if we know our value on an intellectual level, we may not have fully embodied it in our hearts. This book that you hold in your hands exposes the key reasons why we get stuck, and helps unlock for us ways to lay to rest the endless cycle of self-questioning sabotage. Sabotage that can start very early on in childhood.

Speaking of childhood, I met Jeff on the school playground in 1972. Yes, you read that right. We attended the same small private school from kindergarten all the way through 12th grade. You would think we would know each other quite well being in the same class year after year. Yet, when we connected years later, we discovered we both struggled in knowing our true value and identity.

Fortunately, I would embark on discovering God's calling on my life, but I can't help but wonder, what if I would have discovered it sooner? How much more impact could I have had?

In my 25 plus years of business experience I've observed something quite intriguing that shows up again and again. First, most people appear focused on getting things done and being successful, yet at the end of the day they don't know if what they did truly mattered— or if they matter. Second, many people sadly struggle with believing in themselves and wonder if they offer any value. Third, the majority of people spend a lifetime questioning their purpose—or silently wondering what it is.

Do you see yourself in any of those scenarios? I know that at one point I did. It's only in the past ten years that have I found my true calling. But for over thirty years of my life I lacked awareness. Why should anyone have to wait that long?

Who Says So? helps you to see differently and think differently about yourself and the world around you. The author guides you to correct the mis-beliefs you have about your value and how it relates to how you're showing up in life. He helps you identify the areas where you may quietly have patterns of critical thoughts because you've been deeply wounded or experienced trauma.

Self-criticism can directly impact our results and relationships. Did you know that self-criticism has adverse effects on our physical health and mental health too? Did you know we cause our own criticism to perpetuate it because we never meet the standards we put on ourselves? And did you know self-criticism causes internal and often external isolation?

But imagine if there was a guide to help you uncover the critical and limiting thoughts you've been telling yourself. Imagine if you could discover the truth of who you really are, and step into the fullness of who you were created to be. Thankfully, you don't have to imagine it. This book will help you see yourself the way that God, who created you, sees you.

This book helps unlock your world and shows you how you can be a guiding light for others to discover their true value and have a healthy love for themselves. Think about how incredible it would be to inspire others in this way.

It starts with you. The world needs your story of restoration. Your story is meant to be a story of boldness that encourages others to live with clarity. I pray that you honor the journey you are about to embark on and allow this book to be part of your healing and pathway to freedom.

—Barbara Gustavson
Founder, Discover Next Step
Author of *Permission to be BOLD*
discovernextstep.com

INTRODUCTION:
Don't Let Your Heart-breakers Become Spirit-breakers

Certainly, it would seem overly obvious for me to state that this world is filled with heartbreak. As I write, I can think of so many personal stories of heartbreak that have been shared by others. Many have recently lost loved ones, some by natural causes, some by the hand of others, and others by their own hand. Others have hearts that have been broken by those they loved. One woman I met told me her husband announced their divorce to her by email! Many heartaches begin at home with people who are meant to be loving, caring, and protective. Many have turned to religion to help ease their pain. Those people found that conformity to specific traditions and behaviors was demanded in order to find acceptance, rather than an embrace and comfort at their exact point of need

Though individual circumstances vary greatly, I believe every person has experienced heartbreak at some point, some just more so than others. However, heartbreak isn't the most important thing to address when painful and difficult situations come. Pain is to the soul what a cut is to the body. The cut may hurt, but it can be healed if treated appropriately. However, if the cut is left untreated, infection can set in and cause significant, and sometimes fatal damage.

During the Civil War, medicine wasn't nearly as advanced as it is today. Many deaths came not from the injuries the soldiers incurred, but from the infections that entered the wounds. I've read that some infections carried up to a ninety-seven percent mortality rate!

Unfortunately, the same applies to wounds of the soul. Heartbreak can easily break your spirit if left unproperly treated. The messages about our identity and life that can take hold in our minds and hearts can become infections in our souls. These infections can cause untold damage to our thoughts, emotions, relationships, and decisions This can cause us to fall far short of the meaningful and fulfilling life for which we were made.

A rejection, abuse, or disappointment, if left untreated, can leave us believing messages like, "I'll never amount to anything," "I will never find love," "I'm not adequate," "God doesn't love someone like me," or "Life is pointless and disappointing, why bother?" It is messages like these that can become belief systems and can sink into our hearts and minds and poison our lives from the inside out. These thoughts are the real threat to our well-being, far more than any injury or wounding we could experience.

The reason this book was written is to stop heartbreakers from becoming spirit breakers that will keep you from the incredibly meaningful life for which you were created. You stop them by believing in your great worth and value and becoming all that you can be to add value to others. As you read it, may you find newfound freedom in your soul to break the chains of negativity regarding your identity and worth that have come from all the heartbreaking situations present in our world today

CHAPTER ONE:
From the Beginning–The Beautiful You

"If I had words to make a day for you, I'd sing you a morning golden and true. I would make this day last for all time and fill the night with moon shine." Sings the farmer to his pig in the movie "Babe."[1]

A farmer, who has come to see the value of even a pig, takes to song to comfort and speak value into the pig's heart! Of how much greater value are we than a pig, yet how often do we sing or even speak worth into another's heart, or have it spoken into ours?

Have you ever looked deeply into someone's eye and just thought about what it takes to make an eye and what an eye does? The color, the design, the automatically adjusting light aperture (the pupil), which reflects the observer in miniature, are all marvelous works of fantastic and intricate design. Have you considered what it takes to make a cell that can receive light and turn it into a signal that conveys color, texture, and depth to our brain where a picture is formed? From this, we can gather meaning and feelings, have thoughts about, and respond to what is taking place around us.

Have you ever considered that no chemist or biologist with all the world's resources could ever create a living cell from nothing? Yet we are each magnificently composed of vast numbers of these living cells: taking in nutrients, eliminating harmful toxins, allowing for breath, motion, beauty, speech, and art. They work together in the greatest complexity to make us what we are. We are each a miracle of unimaginable worth, yet, how rarely do we truly see it in ourselves.

How critical are we of ourselves, and others? How little do we sense the miracle of what we are? How self-critical are the beautiful, and how hopeless are those who don't recognize their own beauty? How often do we pause and notice the things that make us beautiful, living creatures that, possess a soul, spirit, and body? How often do we appreciate that in others? How appreciated do you honestly feel? How appreciated do others feel when they are around you?

Now let me ask you this: what could be more important?

I was reminded the other day of the words spoken about Joseph and Mary at the time of Jesus' birth, "There was no room for them in the inn." How often have we felt that there is just no room for us in this life? Many situations can make us feel this way; for example, trying to find a parking space, seats at a concert, or waiting in an endless line.

Usually, I feel like I am in someone's way or they are in mine. What has happened? How did we, of immense beauty and breathtaking design, come to this? We are frantic, exhausted, angry, and depressed. Without peace, never truly resting, and never quite feeling safe, no matter how large our assets. How the mighty have fallen. How the beautiful have been stained. We have exchanged that which is most beautiful, most gracious, and most noble for that which matters least and is destined to perish with the using.

Why have we, the glorious ones, placed as head over all creation, sullied ourselves and opted for that which cannot last, instead of living out the miracles we are all meant to be?

When was the last time you saw yourself or another person as the king or queen of this earth that they were meant to be?

When have you ever looked at another and been overwhelmed by their significance, their beauty, and their worth?

Can you see the beauty that you possess, the design beyond compare, a reflection of the image in which you are made?

The ability to recognize beauty is essential to life. Without it, a disesteem will set in that will slowly poison us and will ultimately bring about physical death as well as an inner one. With it, though, our spirits will be lifted. As we see our worth and the worth of those around us, every encounter will take on a new meaning.

We will be granted the privilege throughout each day to interact with others of immense value. We will have the overwhelming opportunity to speak into their lives the worth that they possess, and in offering this to others, we will find the meaning and purpose for which we were made. Someone once said, "The heart of every issue is a heart issue." I would add that at the heart of every heart issue is a relationship, and we were made for relationships.

Dr. Emoto has proven in his magnificent, documented work with water, that even the material universe is affected by the way we think, feel, and speak. Water, when prayed or sung over, takes on beautiful crystalline forms. Even words written on a bottle label can affect the molecular shape of the water in the bottle.

Words such as "Thank you" or the "Chi of love" produce beautiful designs in the water molecules, while words such as "You make me sick; I'm going to kill you," produce ugly, distorted patterns. As Dr. Emoto's work points out if words can have that effect on water, and we are composed mostly of water on the physical level, what impact do words have on us? How can we so lightly esteem that which is created with such design and complexity in another individual? How can we so disesteem it in ourselves?

I love the words of Jesus, in Luke 12:27, "Consider the lilies of the field, they toil not, neither do they spin, but I tell you that even Solomon, in all his splendor was not arrayed like any one of these. If God so clothes the grass of the field, which is here today and tomorrow is thrown into the fire, will He not much more clothe you, oh you of little faith."

Our confidence in God's willingness to take care of us is a very accurate indicator of how much we truly consider ourselves to be worth. Fear, today, as it was in Biblical times, is the telltale indicator of a lack of self-worth. When we fear, we are saying that we do not think we are worth being taken care of and that evil will ultimately be allowed to be visited upon us, resulting in our ultimate demise. Consider if you will, the number of times when you feared the worst, and it did not come to pass. Think of the number of times we have found ourselves in a position beyond our control and worried greatly about it, but in the end, something better than we could have imagined came about.

We worry, yet we have been provided for countless times, even when it was beyond our means to care for ourselves. As the cartoon character Calvin once said, "I think it is dark at night so we can imagine our fears with less distraction!"[2] Oh, how skilled we are at this! Would that we were as skilled at seeing our worth and beauty, the worth and beauty of this breathtaking world and universe, and the others around us!

Think for a moment about what we consider "normal" and take for granted. We live on a planet incredibly suited to sustain life. We have oceans filled with magnificent and frightening creatures. The waves roar, the wind blows, mountains tower, meadows are filled with colors of intense and beautiful hues, the birds migrate and sing, storms howl, thunder rages, and lightning splits the skies. The moon rises, and the sun warms and gives life to all things.

We are currently spinning over 1,000 miles per hour as we rotate on the axis of this planet we call home. Moreover, we are falling about 70,000 miles per hour through space on a phenomenal journey around the sun that we call an orbit. The sun, which we hardly give any thought to, except at a beautiful sunrise or sunset, is a raging ball of fire, as hydrogen is converted into helium at temperatures of about thirteen million degrees Kelvin, and is the size of 333,000 Earths!

The whole solar system is traveling through this universe at an incredible rate of speed. Yet, we can sit on the porch and drink wine from Europe or California, see the colors, feel the breeze, and think it normal! This doesn't even begin to consider the myriad of systems at work in our own bodies, fighting bacteria, moving blood and nutrients, providing sight, touch, smell, taste, and hearing, all of which are essential to our existence.

Does it seem that something has blinded us from seeing reality? Does it appear that maybe we are living on a level far below the awareness of what is truly occurring? Does it seem we have lost our sense of the value of ourselves, others, and this magnificent, beautiful, and sometimes overwhelming universe in which we live? Could we have blocked out anything beyond our control and made God into some passive being that is never bigger than what we are comfortable with and never requires anything from us? His heart is for us to be amazed, overwhelmed, and part of something far more significant and more beautiful than we could ever imagine.

Have we castrated God and made Him tame, never ferocious, passionate, creative, intense, or truly loving? Have we made Him cold, uncaring, untouched by our suffering, and dead? We, as men and women, above all things, are made in His image and to reflect His glory. Our own glory, as well as His, is something beyond us, above us, and something we can never attain. It must be received as a gift. All our striving to hold on to what we think we need, and need to be, will only weary us. Only when we open our hands and release our grip on that which we would cling to and attempt to control, will we ever be able to have poured into our hearts the meaning and worth of who we are, and of what we represent. Only when we open our hearts to realize where we are and who we are, will life open to us. Only then will we begin to truly live.

If I am honest, so many pursuits throughout my life that held the promise of fulfillment, have felt much more like dying than living. So much of what I feared most, as my heart has become open to letting go of control, of being honest, allowing myself to accept who I am, in Whose image I am made, and where I am in this universe at this time; things which I feared would be death, because they forced me to let go of control, have become so much more like living.

APPLICATION EXERCISE:

- Take a few minutes, preferably each day, to think of and write down as many things as you can, that describe your unique design and beauty.

  Maybe your eye and hair color, the five senses that allow you to experience this world in all its richness, your immune system, and your personality and gifting, would be a good place to start.

- Turn these into items for gratitude! No scientist on earth could design you. You are a gift from God. These gifts He has given you give you great potential! No one else has exactly what you do!

NOTES

NOTES

ENDNOTES:

[1] Babe, movie. Universal pictures; Kennedy Miller Productions, 1995. https://www.imdb.com/title/tt0112431/companycredits?ref=ttdtco

[2] Calvin and Hobbes, Bill Watterson. Andrews-McMeel Publishing, 1985-1995, https://en.wikipedia.org/wiki/Calvin_and_Hobbes

CHAPTER TWO:
An Intense Hatred–The War Against Us

"Why does my heart, feel so bad? Why does a soul, feel so bad?" asks songwriter Moby.[1]

Often, I have noticed a recurring theme in movies. The hero is someone the bad guys can't get. He is too smart, to well-equipped to fight them, too skilled, or in some other way out of reach. In these situations, the movie writers often have the bad guys turn to the hero's family to hurt and manipulate the hero. They will kidnap them or threaten them in some way. They know the way to get him under their control is to threaten what he loves most. Another way bad guys sometimes hurt the good guys is to paint a false picture of them to frame them and cause others to distrust them through spreading lying messages about them.

I believe this is such a common theme because it is what is happening in the spiritual realm around us, every day. We are God's beloved, and though His enemy, the devil, cannot overthrow God, he can come against us with lying messages about our worth, get us to make poor choices that result in hurting ourselves and drag us down in an effort to hurt God. Now, I don't believe for a minute that the devil is a little red guy with a pitchfork and tail. No, that is a silly image made to cause us to doubt his very existence.

He is far worse. He attacks us through lies about ourselves and false beliefs about our worth and God's love for us. He attacks and twists everything that is true about our value to God. These are the things that undo our lives if we let them. Let's unpack what this battle looks like in our daily lives.

In the quote at the beginning of this chapter, Moby's

question is a very valid one. What is it that makes us feel so bad? Why is it that we are so depressed that science has now made a huge business of studying brain chemistry to find out how to make drugs to alleviate the feelings of despair and depression so many have? Isn't it that at some deep level, we don't feel understood, appreciated, or that we belong and are loved? Don't we feel like the true us isn't valued, that we aren't genuinely desired for what we really are, or that what we really are isn't worth anything? Isn't that the question that has burned in our souls throughout our lives? Am I truly desirable? Am I truly worth anything? Does the real me matter to anyone?

A question I would like to raise is, if we are truly worth so little, then why is there such a huge campaign throughout our lives aimed at convincing us it is so? Why wouldn't it just be obvious? Who designed this campaign to destroy our sense of value by using other people, and often, those that we love the most to hurt us? Who is it that has told us we are worth so little and who consumes our days on this earth frantically striving to achieve something or reach some level, either socially, personally, or religiously that will bring back the lost sense of worth? Why are we bombarded everywhere we go with subtle, and some not so subtle, messages that we don't measure up?

Why does the guy in the Mercedes seem more valuable than me? Why do I feel better when I see the tabloid in the grocery store telling me that some gorgeous celebrity has gained a few pounds and has cellulite? Is it not because there is comfort in knowing that even those who appear perfect cannot be perfect indefinitely? Eventually, they end up like me, like you, feeling less than desirable, far less than perfect. Why do I feel less valuable when I see People magazine's issue with their picks for the most beautiful people? Why does the person with the beautiful house on the lake seem worth more? Why does a woman with cosmetic surgery feel more desirable?

Why is it that those who attain all society tells them they need to feel worthy, don't? And why is it that those who haven't achieved all those things, still don't feel worthy either? Why is it that no matter how much we've done, or how well we've done, someone or something is always there to remind us of what else needs to be done? How many times have we silenced our hearts, or the honest words to another that we wanted to speak, but were afraid to, because we thought it wouldn't matter, that no one would care what we had to say, or what we felt, or what we thought? What is this emptiness that plagues us, isolates us, demeans us, and makes us feel so very alone? What is truly taking place around us, within us?

I think to fully appreciate what is, and has been occurring in our lives, we must first understand that if a man has an enemy dedicated to his destruction, he will also be devoted to the destruction of the children born from and loved by him. So it is with us. God has an enemy dedicated to His destruction. He made us in His image, so we too have an enemy dedicated to our destruction. The enemy hates God's image because he hates that he cannot be truly loved. It may be helpful to understand that Satan is also referred to as Lucifer, which means "light" or "to shine." It seems clear from many religious traditions, that Lucifer was originally a stunning angel, with a prominent place in creation, who lived in the presence of God. It seems that beauty and the resulting pride were his undoing, and that he like we so often are, was not content just being the recipient of life and love.

He wanted to be the author of life, be praised as such, loved and worshiped, and in doing so, usurping God's glory and throne. He did not understand God's love. The Lord's driving motive is love because it is only love that can have life and create new life, like when a child is conceived from the love of the parents. It is only love that gives glory and creates new life. It is love the knit us intricately and marvelously together in the deep quietness of our mother's womb. It is love that first smiled on us when we were born, and that has been faithfully with us every day—our best and our worst—whether we realized it or not.

Through all of life's suffering, it is important to see that a greater battle is raging. The enemy wants to destroy us using lies. Thankfully, we are also divinely protected, often beyond our knowledge. I believe that if Satan were allowed to actively destroy us, he most certainly would. However, he is restrained by God from doing so outright. He can only do it with our consent.

If we believe a lie about our worth and believe that God doesn't love us, we are bound to seek fulfillment, escape, and pleasure in our own ways. This means we are unwittingly Satan's partner in our own destruction by acting on the lies he has fed us and that we have accepted. God gives us the free will to believe what we will.

By accepting lies about God, and ourselves, from Satan that started in Eden, we have headed down a course to our own destruction. Eve believed she was not worth God giving her His best, often we believe the same. We all try to find fulfillment in our own way, even when it is at the expense of ourselves, our potential, and the best interest of others.

A very real spiritual war is being waged against us each day, right in the middle of our minds, about what we believe is true!"

Join me now as we explore the 'ordinary' ways in which these messages infiltrate our minds and poison our lives. Walk with me on a journey to replace—those messages—with the most fulfilling and freeing truths imaginable. The truths in which you were born to thrive!

APPLICATION EXERCISES:

- My mentor, Paul Martinelli, says that if we talked to others in the ways we talk to ourselves, we'd all be in jail!

    What are some of the things you have told yourself that don't agree with your incredible worth, beauty, design, and potential?

- How have these agreements with damaging beliefs caused you to act in ways that weren't in your own best interest?

- What limiting beliefs, negative self-judgments, and voices of your inner critics have you accepted? What would be the opposite of those messages?

NOTES

NOTES

ENDNOTES:

[1] Why Does My Heart Feel So Bad? Written and performed by Moby, 1999. Label- Mute, https://www.amazon.com/Why-Does-Heart-Feel-Bad/dp/B00002ZZNI

CHAPTER THREE:
Heart Messages, Family, and Abuse

"Dear God, make me a bird so I can fly far, far away."[1]
—*Jenny from Forrest Gump.*

Perhaps you remember Jenny from the movie Forrest Gump. Jenny represents the stories of so many people. She has a terrible, abusive father, and all she wants to do is get away. Jenny is important to Forrest, but she uses destructive behavior to try to escape her past. Forrest tries to erase her pain by getting rid of the house she grew up in, but the memories remain and affect all she does. Many can relate to her story because their lives at home set the stage for a life of pain, lies about themselves, and terrible choices.

> **If home doesn't feel like home, we will search all our lives for a sense of home.**

For the long ages following Eden, the attack against our worth has begun at home. The assault on our worth will often start there and take on many forms. Some are obvious, such as physical, verbal, emotional, or sexual abuse. Others are more subtle, such as making a child believe that they must be achieving something to be worthy. This never allows them to relax and feel loved and appreciated just for who they are. If home doesn't feel like home, we will search all our lives for a sense of home.

If family members act more like strangers, we will search all our lives for intimacy. We are even willing to lose our honor and sense of worth to gain it. If we don't feel valued at home, we will give everything to anyone who promises that to us, regardless of their true motives. If our family does not appreciate us, then we will believe ourselves to be unworthy, spending a lifetime trying to find someone to restore our sense of worth, often defiling ourselves, or pursuing the wrong goals in the process.

What is the essence of good and evil? What is the root of abuse? The essence of good is that it imparts worth and value to a human heart. The nature of evil is that it puts at risk or devalues a human heart, be it our own, or another's. The essence of abuse at the deepest level (many levels can be affected) is that we are made to feel worthless, or at best, worth less. Any activity against us, or another, that makes us feel worth less than what we were made to be, is abuse.

> **What is the essence of good and evil?**

Our hearts remember this, don't they? Why is it that I can't remember much about what I learned in school, but I can remember the little league baseball coach devaluing me with his words. He said, "you aren't worth a hill of beans, go play basketball!" Why was my ability to play baseball associated with my worth as a person? Why is it that someone who is skilled at some sport is often paid enough money to eradicate hunger in many small countries, while the people in those countries are rarely thought of?

What has happened in your life to make you feel like you were worthless or at least worth less? You remember, don't you?

But, do you know that what you were made to feel, was a lie?

My heart especially goes out to the victims of sexual abuse, because of the image it forms in their hearts about themselves and sex and intimacy as a whole. It seems so difficult for a sexual abuse victim to see sex and intimacy together in a healthy way. Often it seems that sex takes on a wild, strictly erotic tone that is far, far removed from any true personal intimacy.

So, on the one hand, there is a feeling of shame for the wild, yet addictive, uncleanness with the sexual partners, while true intimacy occurs only with those whom they consider friends. As a result, they find themselves unable to have true intimacy, which includes their whole person. It is as though the personality is divided, and they live in two different worlds and have a constant fear of the dark one being exposed.

No wonder Jesus said that it is impossible that offenses not come against children, but for those who injure them, it would be better for them if a heavy millstone were hung around their necks and they were drowned in the depths of the sea. I think what abuse victims often see as God not caring, is simply Him giving space for the offender to repent before that final judgment comes. If they do not judge themselves, then the day is coming when it will be done.

I heard of a man whose daughter was raped by two young men. After some time, one of the young men came to her with the greatest humility and from the heart asked her forgiveness, which she granted. The other one refused to repent and later died in a midair collision over Los Angeles. I think this will ultimately be the fate, in some form or another, for all who have inflicted such injuries, yet refuse to recognize the worth of the one(s) they injured.

I believe for the ones who have suffered such injuries, there must be a touch of grace on their hearts, whereby they are restored to a true concept of intimacy. The unclean, wrong view of sex, as developed by the abuse, will have to be understood to be a horrible distortion of what sex was meant to be and sex will have to be seen for the first time as an extension of true intimacy, which occurs first between the hearts of two people who know each other and are committed to loving each other and putting each other and their needs first. They must also realize that though they have been engaged in a horribly wrong physical union with another, it does not make them that type of person.

I have never heard it said but have sometimes wondered if, in the midst of abuse, there can occur some degree of connection of the abused to the abuser, because we are physical and sexual beings, even though the victim knows the event is wrong and should never have occurred. I wonder if then, the sense of connection to the perverse act, which was not their fault, makes them feel that they are a person who is perverse, and they internally take on that identity. No matter what the case, their identity as a person and a sexual being must be healed and their sense of worth be restored in all areas. May God grant this to all the victims of this abuse.

I do not personally believe that there is any human agency, which can bring about this realization. It must be by way of revelation to the heart of the abused, in which the false identity, based on the abuse, is revealed to be a lie, and the true person they were always meant to be, is revealed, adopted, and appreciated.

Now I do not for a minute believe that all the effects of what we have experienced will go away overnight, but I do believe from the bottom of my heart, that if we can emotionally go back to the things that happened in our lives that caused us to feel disesteemed, devalued, or valued for the wrong reasons (such as sexual abuse), or to feel worth less than what we desired, and what we truly are; and if we can see from our hearts that those feelings were based on a lie, communicated in whatever form, by someone who didn't have a clue, or the least bit of understanding of what we were truly worth, that we will begin to be free.

> **At the point where we one day see with complete clarity ... I believe we will be totally free.**

At the point where we one day see with complete clarity the worth that we have always had, I believe we will be totally free. Now what I mean by being free is having the ability to choose the best, the right thing.

Our choices reveal how free, or not, we really are. When we make bad choices, and by that, I mean choices that impact us, or someone else, in some negative way, we are revealing that we do not see our worth clearly.

If we could see our own worth clearly, we would see the worth of others just as clearly and would make decisions that would indicate the worth we saw in ourselves and them, and which would put no one at risk. Until that day, we are becoming more and more free as we see with greater clarity the truth of our worth that we have always had but couldn't see.

It may pay to keep in mind that we can live in two worlds. In one world, we may make decisions that are very destructive and in the other do things that seem incredibly sacrificial and benevolent. Often it seems that this may be a compensation for the guilt acquired from the destructive behaviors, coupled with a deep desire to be a better person and make a real contribution.

This brings us to another issue that we will begin to explore in the family setting, but which will apply to all areas of life as well. This is the issue of forgiveness. Now before you close the book because you couldn't ever dream of forgiving, in the traditional sense, the person who abused you, please let me explain what forgiveness really is. First, let's begin by stating what it is not.

Forgiveness is not saying that what happened was OK!

It is not saying that it was less bad than it was; it is not minimizing the offense in any way or saying that the offender had any right to do what was done!

Forgiveness is recognizing that what the offense made me feel about myself is not true, and I don't have to keep resenting the person who made me feel that way because now I know the truth about my worth!

The offense caused me to feel worth less than I am, and at that time, I couldn't see how much I was worth because the offense hurt so much. However, I have been graciously sustained, often beyond my ability to see. As the familiar poem "Footprints"[2] suggests, during my difficult times, when I saw only one set of footprints as I walked with God and thought I had been abandoned, it was actually then that I was being carried by Him, though I was unaware of it.

Later, I may come to realize that I have been brought to a place where I can see my worth more clearly and see that what happened wasn't a real reflection of me at all. If the truth is known, an offense of any kind doesn't reveal a thing about me, only about my offender. But my, how it so often affects our view of ourselves. What I choose to do as a result is what truly reveals something about me.

In the situation I described earlier, would I believe that I am worthless because I don't know how to play baseball, or would I realize that there was a very immature little league coach who was more concerned with winning a game, so he could have a false sense of worth, than with recognizing the value I had as a human being and working with me to help me get better at baseball, or to find something I was more suited to, while sustaining my sense of worth?

Will you realize that the feelings you had about yourself as the result of your abuse were not a true reflection of who you are, or will you go on feeling that those lies are the truth and resenting, if not hating, the one who caused you to feel what you did? Once we can see how distorted the perspective of the offender was and how valuable we really are, we may actually feel sorrow for their wasted life and desire that they are able to see and be made whole, in order that another life not be wasted. Forgiveness also means stepping down from the throne of judgment and saying, 'I no longer pronounce judgment against you'". This both frees the forgiver from being tied to gaining justice and releases the forgiven to help them see their own value more clearly, and hopefully, the value of others as well, if they choose to. Either way, the forgiver can walk away with a clear conscious, and can stop dragging the past behind them.

Please realize here that I understand that there are those reading these words who have sustained unimaginable forms of abuse and have carried the scars to their self-image and sense of worth for years. It may seem as though it would be unbelievably painful to have to revisit those abuses. Please consider here that there are two types of pain. There is a pain that is temporary and brings gain and relief. There is also a type of pain that is ongoing and only poisons everything else a person ever does. Revisiting an abuse in order to gain a perspective from a more mature point of view that will lead ultimately to freedom and choices that will benefit us and others, is not a bad pain. The pain that comes from the abuse, the resulting false self-image, and the bad choices that will come from it, is a pain to be avoided at all costs.

It has cost enough already, hasn't it?

Must it continue forever while we continue to believe the lie that what we felt about ourselves, due to the abuse, is the truth? One thing is certain; we will have some pain either way. Avoiding thinking about an abuse and the way it made us feel, will only keep the feelings buried, but they will still be there and will poison our lives. As someone has said, 'Any emotion that we bury is buried alive.' The only path to true and lasting healing is to dig it up, expose it to the truth, keep affirming the new messages about our value and worth (see appendix), and let those begin to sink in and change our thinking and our feelings.

As we revisit the old pains and false messages they sent, it will hurt as we realize the way we've been thinking about ourselves all this time and recognize the way it has affected all our decisions and relationships. However, as the truth about our worth replaces the lies, healing will begin to come. As the healing comes, we will make better decisions and will, as a result, experience better situations and dynamics in all areas of our lives. As these things continue and bring a positive aspect to our lives, we will realize more fully than ever that the lies we believed about ourselves, were in fact lies, and as we see our true selves emerging, and begin to realize that we never have to live the way we have for so long ever again, we will experience a new joy in life and will eventually be able to help others experience the same.

Each of us carries within us a message that can change the world for the better, if we will learn what it is that we truly are and see the abuses as a means to realize all that we have always been, but couldn't see, and all that we can be. In this way, God truly acts as the divine Kung Fu artist, taking the worst assaults on our self-image, sustaining us through the misery, while we can't see the truth, and then bringing us to a realization of a truth that is more incredible than anything we could have ever experienced if the abuse hadn't pushed us to reach more firmly for reality and truth than ever before. In this way, we can also be ministers of value to other people. As we recognize their value, which we didn't see before, we help them on their journey toward wholeness and believing the truth also. This adds even more to our own sense of value, as we help others forward in their healing process.

Evil will not ultimately win unless we give in to it and choose to believe that a lie is true.

Again, I do not expect those scars to heal in an instant. What I beg you to do, though, is to revisit the events and to ask one question; What did this make me feel about myself, about my worth as a person, about who I am?

The more honestly we can answer this question, the more of a chance we have to heal because we can begin to realize that what we felt about ourselves as a result of the abuse and what the truth about us is, are two utterly different things. It is possible to live our entire lives believing a lie and suffering throughout our entire existence as a result. However, it is also possible to realize that the things we believed about ourselves are a lie and to replace that lie with the truth that we are valuable and loved beyond imagination and that anyone who makes us feel it isn't so is living in the dark and lies until now.

In the quest for freedom, it is also important that we receive forgiveness from those we have devalued since none of us are free from devaluing others in some way. Asking forgiveness is as simple as realizing that in some way, we didn't value someone at the level they deserve as human beings, made in God's image. When we recognize this and ask their forgiveness, we are saying that we now realize the value they truly have and realize that we were wrong in undervaluing them previously.

The really nice thing about this is that it places us back in agreement with God about the worth of the other people and frees us from having to live with the guilt of our wrong and also from the blame we usually place on them to justify our actions. It is so natural and easy to blame someone else for our own wrongs against them. When we do this though, we must continually rehearse in our own minds what we believe is wrong with them, in order to ease our own sense of guilt, which is never released by blaming others. To rid ourselves of this guilt/blame cycle, we must own our responsibility to seek forgiveness, see their value in God's eyes, and forgive them for any true offenses as well. It is extremely important, however, to seek forgiveness because we truly see the worth of the other person and how we have devalued them, not simply because we want to feel better ourselves, by alleviating our own guilt.

APPLICATION EXERCISES:

- Whether you had a solid, affirming family that valued you highly or were one of the many who did not, think of the primary messages that you received about your value when you were growing up.

- How did those messages make you feel?

- How did you respond to those feelings?

- What results of your choices, based on your feelings, did you get?

- The Law of Polarity says that for every thought you can imagine, there is another thought that is its polar opposite. Use this to record what all the positive thoughts look like, that are the opposite of the negative thoughts and feelings you have had in the past. Use this list of positives to think on and reflect on. Put yourself in those images and let them sink in, replacing the negative thoughts and feelings. For example, if you always felt you would be a failure at something you wanted to do and therefore never tried it, picture yourself doing the very thing you believed you could not do and succeeding. The more you picture yourself in this way, the more you will begin to identify with the right beliefs and what they look like when put into practice. Also, choosing to be around others who believe in you and your visions and who can support you in your growth will be a huge help in moving forward. If the wrong people can cause us to believe lies, the right people can certainly help us believe the truth! This practice, over time, will transform your belief system and help restore a positive self-image, resulting in much better choices and results.

Note: In the References and Appendices sections at the end of this book is a list of truths about your identity in God's eyes. There is also a table for you to write the beliefs which you have held as well as the truth of who God says you are. Replacing one with the other has resulted in newfound freedom, good decisions, and good results for millions of people around the world.

NOTES

NOTES

ENDNOTES:

[1] Forrest Gump, movie. Paramount Pictures (presents) (A Steve Tisch/Wendy Finerman Production by) (A Robert Zemeckis Film), 1994. https://www.imdb.com/title/tt0109830/

2 Footprint in the Sand, poem. Mary Fishback Powers. https://www.onlythebible.com/Poems/Footprints-in-the-Sand-Poem.html

CHAPTER FOUR:
Heart Messages and Social Interaction

"Subdivisions, in the high school halls, in the shopping malls, conform or be cast out. Subdivisions, in the basement bars, in the backs of cars, be cool or be cast out."[1]

—*Rush*

For many of us, social interactions have formed a large part of our identity. What we perceive to be our identity, based on how others see us and treat us, can determine how we perceive ourselves and live our lives, if we let it. If we believe we aren't worth much in the eyes of others, we may not try to do much, play small, and get small results, never reaching our potential and greatest impact. School has been a place of significant growth and learning for some; for others, it was a place of being devalued and bullied, sometimes creating scars that have lasted for a long time, maybe even a lifetime.

How I can identify with the cartoon character Calvin of Calvin and Hobbes, who called P.E. class "contemporary studies in state sponsored terrorism."[2] School seemed that way in general. Forced to pay so much attention to things we cared about so little, while we were demeaned for the things we cared about so much, and which weighed so heavily on our hearts. As Guy Doud, author of Molder of Dreams[3], points out, who cares about split infinitives when a family is broken and with it the hearts of the kids caught in the middle. How often have we been forced by society to focus on trivialities and things we couldn't care less about, while the weighty issues of our hearts and lives have gone unaddressed? Grammar and math hold very little value to a heart that lives in a broken home, or one with abuse, or any number of other heartbreaking things which can go on in a "home." How wonderful it would be if all teachers could see the hearts of the children they teach and help heal the heart issues before trying to teach other trade skills. Thank God for the teachers who do see great value in others, and have made such a difference for so many.

For most of us, school is the beginning of our social interaction on any real level. I would say that what we learn from this interaction is the real lesson of school, while all the facts are just what we need (or often don't need) to know to make some money and have a decent life. Our current school model was designed to create workers during the industrial revolution, not to create people who see their value and understand how to develop themselves to make the unique contribution to the world that only they can make.

May I Ask What You Learned In School?

My first day of school taught me that I was different. I was four years old and had no idea where I was or why I was there. I didn't know anyone. I was lying alone by the baseboard heater under a window, just watching what was going on, when Miss Meyers came to me, leaned over, and said, "Don't you like to play with cars? I've never seen a little boy that didn't like to play with cars!" I couldn't have given a rip about cars and would have liked to have told her so, but thankfully, something told me that wasn't a good idea!

So, my very first day of Kindergarten, I learned that something was different about me, and something about me seemed to be wrong. Later, I learned many other things. I learned that I was fat and that it isn't OK at all to be fat, especially if it rains outside and you have to share the gym with the girls and play basketball on the "skins" team, which I always seemed to get chosen for. My way of coping with the embarrassing situation was to move as little as possible so that I didn't draw attention to my fat and myself. I had no one who understood or was able to help with my dilemma, so I would mope through the rest of the day in shame feeling rejected and unwanted, then come home and eat ice cream to feel better. You can see the cycle here, right?

As much as I have learned since then, there are still a few "coaches" (and I use the term loosely) I would dearly love to slap upside the head for their ignorant insensitivity. I also learned that to be cool, you had to have Nike or Converse basketball shoes. You didn't dare wear "bobos" on the court; everything had to be approved by a self-appointed council of peers!

I would have loved to have had a headmaster like the one in the movie Cider House Rules. Remember the evening scenes, just before "lights out," when the headmaster would visit the boys as they were going to bed? Each evening, just before turning out the lights, he would say, "Goodnight, you princes of Maine, you kings of New England." One evening, after the lights were off, one boy asks another, "Why does he always say that?" "Because he knows we like it."[4] was the response. Having an esteemed figure speak value into our hearts is a gift like no other! Often, having just one person who sees our worth, our potential, and a beautiful picture of the future for us can change everything. I serve on the board of an advocacy center for people with disabilities. As I've heard many incredible stories of those who have moved past their disabilities and accomplished great things, one thing stands out. Often in the midst of ridicule by others and personal depression, it was a single figure who made all the difference in their lives by believing in them, seeing value in them, and always encouraging them to move forward." May we each be such a figure for someone.

How our mood is lifted by a moment of appreciation or praise. In this age of disesteem, we hold the most valuable treasure at the tip of our tongues, the power to bring dignity and worth to another human being. How one word of gratitude, or appreciation, can lift our spirits after so many negative messages we live with every day, often just taken as the norm, as we have become so accustomed to them. "Sticks and stones may break my bones, but words will never hurt me." Yeah, right! What a lie that turned out to be. We are affected our entire lives by words. King Solomon had it right, "Life and death are in the power of the tongue."

I can vividly remember the worth I felt when Dr. Baxter told me in an English class, "it's nice to have a student who understands what we're talking about." Finally, someone saw some worth in me and pointed it out. I identified with that and felt great pride in it for many years. However, I can also remember, just as vividly, the shame I felt when a man I greatly respected publicly questioned my identification of a Black-tailed

Gnatcatcher, on a birding trip to Texas. The interesting thing is, I'll bet neither of them knew they affected me in any way.

What then is at the heart of the abuse most of us have suffered while in school? What is the question that is truly being asked in the hearts of all of us, all the time? Isn't the burning question in all our social interactions, "What does it take to be somebody of worth?" "What does it take to be recognized, valued, and loved?"

Why else do we spend so much money on clothes, makeup, perfumes, colognes, and cars?

Why do we feel we need so much "bling, bling?"

Why do we spend so much time in front of the mirror before going out, or not go out because we feel we cannot make a good enough impression, no matter how hard we try?

One attractive female friend of mine once told me that women look at other women more than men do. I asked why this is, and she responded that they want to know what they are up against. For all of us, it appears that there is a constant comparison of ourselves to others. I mentioned this phenomenon to another female friend, and she responded that she does that too. She is always looking at other women to see if they look good or have nice boobs or butts. If they do, she wishes she had theirs. Any time someone else seems to look better than us, it is easy to feel a slight bit of devaluing, of not being worth as much as they are.

We are taught at a very early age to compare ourselves to others to find out what we are worth. If we learn that people are attracted to us because of our appearance, athletic ability, intelligence, family status, or some other thing, then we feel that we have worth, at least on some level. This false sense of worth usually turns to pride and a demeaning attitude toward those who are not as fortunate as we consider ourselves to be. If we learn that we are looked down on because of our lack of these things, then we may well come to believe that we have no worth. The sad reality is that once someone comes to believe that they lack worth, they most often begin to act like they have no value.

The more they act like they have no worth, the more they are treated like it, since many people cannot see the worth of another apart from actions, and the cycle becomes a huge downward spiral. Unless someone intervenes and can help them see that they have worth, regardless of their abilities, social status, appearance, or anything else, the long-term effects will be devastating.

We each have worth because we are who we are, not because of any other thing! The gifts we possess are only mediums, through which we are to convey worth to others or use to beautify the world, bringing joy to others and glory to the God who created it all in the first place and Who gave us the ability to appreciate it and share it with everyone else. Control is an illusion created in the minds of those who cannot see reality. Reality reveals our ultimate inability to do or have anything, apart from the gifts and influence of God and others. Humility is the garment that beautifies those who realize that all they have is a gift beyond deserving, given for their enjoyment and the blessing of others.

Socially, what is it that we all truly want? Do we not desire the attention, approval, and appreciation of all other people? Elaine once asked George on Seinfeld, "Does everyone have to like you?" George's honest answer was, "Yes!"[5]

Of Course, It's What We Are Made For!

Now let me paint a beautiful picture. Consider that each of us, in our own hearts, becomes convinced of our worth, just because we are who we are. Once that occurs, we will see that our value is based on being human, made in God's image, being deeply loved by Him, and nothing else. We will also realize that each other person is of great worth for the same reasons, and we will appreciate and value them and what each person has to offer from their own unique personality and aptitudes.

When this happens, we will see them with value and appreciation. In this way, we would each have all the positive attention from all the others around us, all the time. What a marvelous world this would then be! One in which no one felt devalued, ever. Can you picture it? Then God would get the glory for being so incredible, and for making us in the first place, with such beauty and design, and giving us such an amazing world, filled with such incredible people, and such love, to live in! I believe this was His original intention and that He will not stop until this vision is realized.

Now that will be a day worth waiting for!

APPLICATION EXERCISES:

- What messages about your worth have you received from others in social interactions?

- What messages are you passing on to others?

- How would you have liked to have been treated and made to feel about yourself?

- How can you pass this on to those around you today?

- Remember the Golden Rule, which says, "Do unto others as you would have them do unto you."

- My mentor, John Maxwell, says that in order to have our best day ever, we must do 5 things:[6]

  1. Value people- before you do anything, see others with the same value with which you want to be seen.

  2. Think of ways to add value to others - think about what is coming up in your day and find ways that you can lift others higher.

  3. Look for ways to add value to others - each day presents us with unique opportunities to add value to others in some way. Look for these and be ready to act when the opportunity arises.

  4. Do things that add value to others - Once you have thought about, and become open to looking for ways to add value, just do it… add the value!

5. Reflect on how you added value to others - each evening, spend a few minutes remembering what you did that day to add value to others. It will help inspire you to do more and also raise your own self-image, by seeing the difference you make in other lives!

Think about the things you like in other people and the way they treat you.

Take a minute to make a list of these things.

Now think about how you can treat others in the same way you like being treated!

NOTES

NOTES

ENDNOTES:

1 Subdivisions, song. Lyrics Neal Peart, performed by Rush, 1982. https://www.imdb.com/title/tt5859724/

2 Calvin and Hobbes, Bill Watterson. Andrews McMeel Publishing, 1985-1995. https://en.wikipedia.org/wiki/Calvin_and_Hobbes

3 Molder of Dreams, book. Guy Doud. Focus on the Family, 1990. https://www.amazon.com/Molder-Dreams-Guy-Rice-Doud/dp/1561790273/ref=sr_1_1?keywords=molder+of+dreams&qid=1556122143&s=gateway&sr=8-1

4 Cider House Rules, movie. Film Colony, Miramax, Nina Saxon Film Design, 1999. https://www.imdb.com/title/tt0124315/

5 Seinfeld, miniseries. West Shapiro, Castle Rock Entertainment, 1989-1998. https://www.imdb.com/title/tt0098904/companycredits?ref=ttdtco

6 John Maxwell, author, speaker. https://en.wikipedia.org/wiki/John_C._Maxwell, www.johnmaxwell.com, https://www.youtube.com/watch?v=ljIzuzOkhnM

CHAPTER FIVE:
Heart Issues and Career

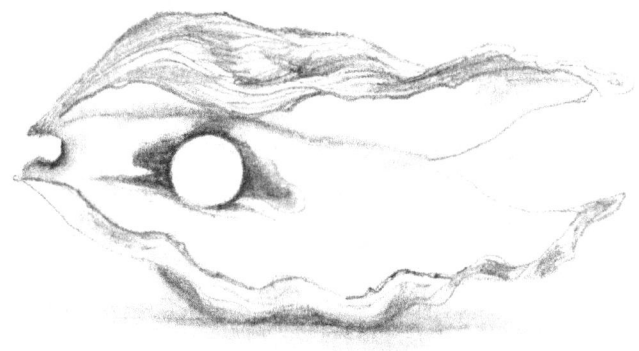

"I'm tired of standing in line to clubs I'll never get in, it's like the bottom of the ninth and I'm never gonna win. This life hasn't turned out quite the way I want it to be."[1]

—Nickleback

"Another day as drab as today is more than a man can endure."[2]

—Rush

Most of us will spend over 11,000 days working during the course of our careers. Since we spend so much of our lives at our jobs, it is well worth understanding why we do what we do for a living and understanding the value it adds to others. It is also well worth exploring why we are doing what we do and see what we have believed about ourselves and our ability to do the things that really matter to us.

"Working 9 to 5"[3] may be a way to make a living, but it is not a way to see our true worth. It also won't help us see the message that has been forming in our hearts throughout our lives. The workplace can help us share that message with others, impacting the world around us positively and giving us fulfillment in the benefit of others as we share our unique vision and gifts with those whom we serve.

As Meg Ryan quoted in the movie Joe vs. The Volcano, "My father says that almost the whole world is asleep… He says that only a few people are awake and they live in a state of constant, total amazement."[4] How many are there who are sleeping? How many go through each day, plodding through the daily routine, never seeing the value they could add to those around them, the value of those around them, and their own value as well?

May I ask how you came to be in your current vocation? Was it a dream that you pursued, or was it more of an accident that happened? Either way, are you fulfilled now, knowing that you can offer something of value, not only by way of goods or service to others, but also of yourself as you do what you do? Do you know that not only is your warm body needed on your job but so is your heart?

I often drive further and pay more to shop at a store, or eat at a restaurant, where I know I will be treated as if I matter, which I do! What price can be set on treating someone with dignity and value? What would the worth of an education be which taught that? Yet all of us, every day, have the opportunity to learn the worth we have ourselves, as well as the opportunity to teach someone else their worth through our words, attitudes, actions, motives, and spirit toward them.

Carpe Diem, seize the day! Make it a better world for someone to live in, as you build worth into their lives. Make them better people for having known you, and yourself a better person for having valued them! Do you know that at this very moment, in whatever vocation you currently find yourself in, that you have been uniquely placed in a situation that will occur exactly once in all eternity and that only you can impact those around you in exactly the way that you can? Do you realize that everyone around you is a living, breathing Rembrandt of value that cannot be estimated and that each moment with them holds an opportunity to regard them as such, and in doing so, impact their lives and the lives of all they will touch, forever?

We are being given moments of rarest value at every point in our lives. What a tragedy to waste them. Each moment and each person is a gem of greatest worth. No wonder Jesus likened the kingdom of heaven to a merchant seeking valuable pearls, who, finding one of great value, sold all that he had and bought it. Do you know that you are that pearl that God gave everything He had to gain? Do you realize that everyone around you is equally as valuable?

We are living a miracle. We are presented with opportunities of greatest worth, and we get paid to have them and to provide a service or product to someone along the way! Of course, the more of our God-given gifts we are using in our vocation, the better we'll be able to add value to our colleagues and our clients. It pays to know our strengths and to develop them to their greatest potential and service to others!

Additionally, each of us holds in our hearts a story and a lesson that will never be duplicated throughout all eternity. No one will ever have the experiences we have had. No one will ever feel exactly what we have felt or be able to communicate it in exactly the same way we can. Each of us holds in our hearts a message, unique to us; that can impact the world around us in a way that no one else can. We must fight the tendency to be so busy that we cannot give or receive the messages that have been placed in our hearts throughout our lives, and in the hearts of others.

> **When we know that someone knows us, understands us, and loves us, loneliness will be banished.**

What is the root cause of loneliness? Is it not that no one really knows us and understands our story? When we know that someone knows us, understands us, and loves us, loneliness will be banished. We are given the opportunity each day to banish loneliness in others. As we seek to know and understand their stories, and as we share our stories, loneliness will be banished. Belonging, connection, and understanding will be restored.

If each of us could know everyone else's story in full depth, we would be enriched beyond imagining. As we share our story, we enrich others and take our part in the great dance of life and make our contribution, without which, life and eternity will never be what it should. In some jobs, there is opportunity to find out a lot about others; in other jobs, this opportunity doesn't exist to any significant degree, but if we realize that each person has a story of infinite value and treat them as such, the world will be a better place because we went to work today! One thing is certain, every person we will ever meet has a story that matters just as much to them, as yours does to you, and mine does to me! Enhancing that story with a sense of value gives great meaning to any work that is done.

It seems that many people today try to find worth in what they do, as opposed to who they are. The tiring, but common, introduction of ourselves turns its focus almost immediately to what we do, not who we are, beyond the statement of our name.

To be sure, many, many careers offer very valuable and worthy services. I am privileged to know so many people working in careers where this is true. But there is a huge problem if we try to base our worth on our job, rather than how we do our job and the value we add through it. I often see people, who appear to be able-bodied, yet are homeless, or asking others for money.

I have often wanted to say to them that if they would just find some job, no matter how insignificant they think it is, and do that job the best they know how, with the best attitude they can have toward the others they will be around, that it will only be a matter of time before they are noticed and other opportunities will be opened for them. For it is not what we do, but how we do it and who we are while doing it, that matters most.

A good friend of mine was awarded a huge contract with no competition, because of the way she saw others as valuable. She was invited to bid on a coaching job in Canada. The organization had branches across the country and was looking for bids from multiple coaches to train in various branches. My friend was invited to meet with them and the other coaches and to present bids.

While she was working a man came to the door of her office. After noticing him, he called her by name, saying how good it was to see her again. She didn't remember who he was and when she asked him, he told her he was the janitor there and that they had spoken several years earlier when she saw him and engaged him in conversation. His memory of their earlier encounter touched her, and she invited him and his wife to dinner that evening.

As she was getting ready to leave the office for the day, the Vice President of the company came to her office door and told her that he was meeting with all the other coaches for dinner and asked if she could join them? She knew how important this was, but also realized her commitment to dinner with the janitor. She asked the V.P. if they could meet the next day, as she already had dinner plans. That evening, she took the janitor and his wife to dinner and had a wonderful evening.

The following morning the V.P. came back to her office and noticed a collection of mementos accumulating around the edge of her desk. He asked about them, and she told him they were tokens of friendship that the janitor had been bringing her, having remembered her from another time at that building. The V.P. said that he knew the janitor, and that he met him on his way into the building that morning and knew where she had been for dinner the night before! He went on to say that they were awarding her the entire national contract to coach their team since she was exactly the type of person they wanted training their people!

Just like my friend, we never know what doors will open to us, as we see others with value and treat them that way, even when it might cost us. Later, that same organization instituted an outstanding customer service and loyalty award to be given annually to a team member. The award was named after the janitor, my friend was at the conference to give the janitor the first of these awards!

I imagine that most employers would far rather have a diligent, positive employee with no formal training, but who is able and willing to learn, than a highly educated, but proud person who doesn't appreciate others because they can't see past themselves! Who would you rather work with? Who would you rather have work for you?

My father caused me to love the saying, "Today is the first day of the rest of your life." No matter if our current vocation is the fulfillment of a vision we've carried since childhood, or if we stumbled into what we are doing now and have no idea where it will lead, we all have the opportunity to do our best today. We can also rest assured, if we do, we will be benefiting not only ourselves but also those that we work for and with, as well as those for whom we are providing goods and services.

Recently I read an article that shared the results of a recent survey of 5,000 people from the U.S., U.K, Germany, and France. The survey found that 56% of people surveyed rank a company's culture as more important than salary! They also found that 73% of the respondents wouldn't even apply to a company unless the company values aligned with their own. This is a huge indicator of how much difference, culture, attitude, and value mean to people.

As Dr. Francis Schaeffer titled his book, there are "No Little People."[5] There are also no little jobs, when that job is done from the heart, with a sense of self-worth, and a vision of the worth of the others around us. As we pursue our careers from this standpoint, we will ultimately be led to that which will be most fulfilling for us personally and be the greatest blessing to others. As we continually develop ourselves to be the best we can be and pass along that value to others, doors will open that we never dreamed of, and opportunities arise for us, just because of the type of people we are!

APPLICATION EXERCISES:

- What do you love to do so much that you would do it for free? This is key to what really motivates you.

- Where can you apply this motivation in your current work to add value to others?

  For example, my motivator is lifting people to a greater awareness of their value. So, wherever I am, I can treat people and discuss things that help them see themselves as being very valuable. The more "meaning markers" (those things that you value and that motivate you), that you can find and add to each day, the better each day will become!

- How can you add value to those who have positions above you? Beneath you? Beside you?

- Here are some ways to help add value to others:

  1. Show sincere appreciation for the services and attitudes of those around you.
  2. When you see others showing particular skills, make mention of how good they are.
  3. Believe in them and what they can do.
  4. Share useful resources with them, to help them grow.
  5. Encourage them during times of failure and help them to see ways to learn from it.
  6. Take time to listen to them to understand where they are and what they need.

NOTES

NOTES

ENDNOTES:

[1] Rockstar, song. Nickelback, 2005, https://www.amazon.com/Rockstar-Explicit/dp/B0011Z0YR2/ref=sr11?keywords=rockstar+nickelback&qid=1556122828&s=gateway&sr=8-1

[2] Middletown Dreams, song. Lyrics by Neal Peart, performed by Rush, 1985. https://www.rush.com/songs/middletown-dreams/

[3] 9 to 5, song. Dolly Parton, 1980. https://www.azlyrics.com/lyrics/dollyparton/9to5.html

[4] Joe vs the Volcano, movie. Warner Brothers, Amblin Entertainment, 1990. https://www.imdb.com/title/tt0099892/

[5] No Little People, book. Francis Shaeffer, 2003. https://www.amazon.com/Little-People-Introduction-Udo-Middelmann-ebook/dp/B0026IUO82/ref=sr_1_fkmrnull_1?crid=3TKMEAD95TOSA&keywords=no+little+people+schaeffer&qid=1556125013&s=gateway&sprefix=no+little+people%2Caps%2C221&sr=8-1-fkmrnull

CHAPTER SIX:
Heart Issues and Relationships–The Devaluing of Women and the Lostness of Men

"Crying on the corner, waiting in the rain, I swear I'll never, never wait again, you gave me your word, but words for you are lies…I'm gonna harden my heart, I'm gonna swallow my tears, I'm gonna turn and leave you here."[1]

—Quarterflash

The devaluing of our hearts and worth by a lover is one of the greatest of all heartaches. Those who have known the intimacy of softly spoken words of affection, the romance of candlelight and wine, the exhilaration of being touched, connected, known in soul and body, of belonging to another and feeling that you hold a special place in their heart that no one else can fill, only to later hear "This isn't working out for me right now," "I'm not in love with you anymore," "I need some space," or "I've found someone else," know like no one else, the devastation of feeling that you don't have what it takes, that you are not enough, that you are not worthy of another's love and devotion.

It is utterly devastating to realize that the plans you made and the dreams you shared didn't matter to the one you loved. You were being played, lied to, and used. It cuts us to the heart. It reduces all we value to insignificance. It reduces us to insignificance. It says we don't matter, that our dreams don't matter, that our hearts aren't valuable. It shatters our souls and destroys our hope. It leaves us alone, broken, very needy, and fearful to ever trust again.

No wonder that the easiest escape route is to harden our hearts. To compound our problem, we often use anger and bitterness, escapism through drugs and alcohol, or illicit affairs with no hope of anything, just going through the motions with no heart involved in an attempt to numb our pain. The word tragic does not begin to capture the loss here. I know of no word that does.

"Trust is just as rare as devotion,"[2] writes Neal Peart of Rush. How difficult is it to look another in the eye and say from the bottom of our heart, in all sincerity, "I love you." How hard is it to believe it when we hear it? Why are they saying that? What do they really mean? What do they really want? If they really knew me, would they say that? Are they really saying they are using me to love themselves?

After all the criticism, heartache, and disappointment we've encountered from those we have loved, how can we truly trust that someone could know us and truly love us? Who can fully know us and value us is our heart's deepest question? Often, the sad conclusion we reach is that no one could fully know us and also deeply love us. What then are we to do?

Modern society has taught us to conceal the real us beneath a cleverly devised illusion of being "OK" and never let anyone near our hearts. "Pay no attention to that man behind the curtain"[3] becomes our subconscious motto. On the one hand, we are exhausting ourselves trying to maintain a facade to convince everyone that what we think they will appreciate and love is what we really are. On the other hand, the real us, while chained in the basement of our hearts and fed the crumbs of what is left over after our wearying attempt at appearing together, is still crying out to be rescued, to be known, to be loved.

In our hopelessness, we turn to illicit affairs, selling ourselves, our souls, and defiling our spirits and bodies in the hope of an easy escape from that which causes so much pain. Eventually, our own addictions cause us to believe more firmly than ever, that we are unlovable, that we are unclean, that we cannot be restored, that we are worthless for anything other than a fleeting moment of pleasure and a life of hopelessness and worthlessness, feeling that being loved by someone both tender and true could never happen to us.

We are assaulted with the double blow of the loss of worth imparted to us by others in our past, and the lies about our worth associated with it, coupled with our moral failures, which gives convincing evidence to our already staggering souls that we are truly worthless. . .hopeless. So we go from one affair to the next, or sometimes multiple ones at once, distracting ourselves from contemplating the situation as it truly is with busyness, or substance abuse, wondering why we can never seem to find fulfillment and end up with large numbers of the population being prescribed antidepressants to be able to make it through today or face another one.

I have often wondered what the defining characteristic of a man is. What is it that makes us men? What is it that we are designed to be and be about? I have known many men that believe it is about how much they can bench press. Many believe true greatness is manifest by athletic prowess, or how many women they can seduce. These things have, for many years, seemed to me to be lacking something vital, something essential to truly being what we were intended to be as men. Recently, it came to my heart very strongly to go back and read about the Mighty Men of many years ago, a story I had not thought of in years, but one that I could not resist the pull to revisit for a clue as to what it is to be a mighty man.

In the Old Testament, we read about a king of Israel named David. His secret service, at the time, was a group of valiant men commonly referred to as Mighty Men. We are told that on one occasion, an invading army came against them when they were near a barley field. All their countrymen fled, but these three Mighty Men took their stand in the field of barley and defended it against the invaders.

If the Mighty Men of that day were concerned with a field of barley and protecting it, how much more should we be concerned with the protection of what really matters? What does this tell us about what it truly is to be a mighty man? Is it not in protecting something of value? Fighting for something that matters, the things that matter most?

In the movie The Matrix Reloaded, Neo is seeking the oracle to find out what he is to do. When he gets close to finding her, he encounters a man named Seraph. After a phenomenal martial arts fight, Seraph tells Neo that he had to be sure he was the One. Neo asks what Seraph is, and his response is, "I protect that which matters most."[4]

Now What is it That Really Matters Most?

If we follow the account of creation as outlined in the Bible, there appears a deepening complexity of life with each new thing created. We move from the material universe where chemicals act and react to form a phenomenal world. Next we see the emergence of actual life, no longer merely chemical equations without life dynamic. The plant kingdom emerges, then animal life, and ultimately us, the crown of all creation, made in the image of God Himself and bearing His glory. Made to rule in beauty, strength, kindness, understanding, and grace.

Filled with wonder and awe at all that we are and this most incredible creation that we are so privileged to be a part of. Man is created first and reflects the majesty and strength and understanding of God. But, the creation is incomplete. The man is alone and not fulfilled. Something very significant is missing. So God places man in a deep sleep and from his rib crafts the last and greatest of His creations. He creates woman.

Let That Meaning Sink In

He creates woman and pours into her soul, heart, and body; all that is beautiful, all that is tender, nurturing, elegant, glorious, and gracious. She is the one who will inspire kings, poets, armies, and artists for all time. The one who can bring life into the world and nurture it into health, fullness, and glory. She is the one for whom wars will be waged, whom men will dream about, for whom they will risk their lives. She brings meaning, beauty, and grace to the world. She is the embodiment of the glory of God. It will be in the heart of every man to win her, to love her, to fight for her, to protect her and cherish all she is, to be captivated by her, and to do all for her good; to protect that which matters most.

But what has happened? Why is it that instead of valuing and protecting women, men have turned to using them to love themselves, to abusing their beauty in a futile effort to regain a sense of their own lost masculinity? Instead of fighting to protect women, men have turned to taking advantage of them, devaluing their nature, their beauty, their hearts, their dreams, and all that is tender, lovely, nurturing, and graceful in this world — leaving them alone, broken, feeling ashamed, unclean, very unlovely, and unlovable.

In the meantime, the degradation of women to regain a lost sense of masculinity has failed to make men feel like men. A man may brag to his friends about all the impure things he did with some desirable woman, but in his heart, he knows that he has failed. He has failed to protect that which matters most. He has failed to fight, to stand, to properly value that which is most valuable, and he has become more lost, more desperate, more needy, weaker. He has become less a man and more an animal, more a creature of need, without purpose, potential, or vision.

> **He has become less a man and more an animal, more a creature of need, without purpose, potential, or vision.**

Now both he and the woman he was to protect, need their worth restored. Now both of them need restoration from the lies they believed about their worth in the first place, and the wrong they did to try to comfort themselves and prove the original lie about their worth incorrect. I think this is what it means to be lost, with no one and nothing, inside this box of our existence in this world to be able to offer a resolution.

In this condition, we must have help from outside of this box. We must be forgiven so profoundly, and loved so deeply, that we are restored from the inside out.

Thankfully, just such help is on the way!

APPLICATION EXERCISES:

- Many lies about our worth can come from the hands of one we love. Most of us, like myself, have been on both the receiving and the giving end of this problem.

- As you think back on what others have done to you, try to identify the messages that were communicated, even if they were never clearly verbalized.

- Think about how it is impossible for someone who cannot see your worth, to ever treat you in a way that truly shows your worth.

- Recognize that their failure to value you as you should be is because they lacked vision of who they, and you, truly are, and the value you have.

- Make a list of the opposite messages from the ones you have received. Write them down. Post them in a visible place. Daily read them, say them out loud. Picture them in your mind, and see yourself as that person of great value, thinking and acting like a person of great value!

Remember, "What we behold, we become." So let those old experiences and messages be your springboard to thinking new thoughts and messages. Each time they arise, remind them of the truth about yourself and your true value!

NOTES

NOTES

ENDNOTES:

[1] Harden My Heart, song. Written by Marv Ross, performed by Quarterflash, 1981. https://en.wikipedia.org/wiki/Harden_My_Heart

[2] Emotion Detector, song. Lyrics by Neal Peart, performed by Rush, 1985. https://www.rush.com/songs/emotion-detector/

[3] Wizard of Oz, movie. Metro-Goldwyn-Mayer, 1939. https://www.imdb.com/title/tt0032138/

[4] The Matrix Reloaded, movie. Warner Bros., Village Roadshow Pictures, Silver Pictures, NPV Entertainment, Heineken Branded Entertainment, 2003.

CHAPTER SEVEN:
Heart Issues and Religion

The aim of most religious systems is manipulating behavior through some means of motivation.

Usually, this happens by creating a feeling of unworthiness and urging people to become more worthy by behaving better. Better behavior, however, is a by-product of having a sense of worth restored, not a means to it. Think about motivation on the job. I read an article recently that stated 50% of workers said they would work for less money if they could work for a better boss! What does this mean? A better boss would be one who gets to know their people, praises their strengths, shows appreciation for their accomplishments, and provides opportunities for growth. Bad bosses are the ones you never hear from unless you've done something wrong. How demotivating is that?

It's much more demotivating when it's done in God's name, as though He is the one finding fault and demanding improvement with a solemn stare. Shaming and fault-finding in an attempt to get them to be better people is a major failure of religion. Having one's flaws pointed rarely motivates anyone toward better behavior.

If the vision of what a person was created to be can be restored, their self-appreciation, appreciation of others, and appreciation of God will make them not want to damage themselves or others. If they don't believe anyone has worth, then what does it matter how anyone is treated. How we treat ourselves, and others, is the tell-tale sign of how much we think we are worth, how much we truly believe that we and others matter.

No matter what a person's theological doctrine is, it

is only be worth as much as how they treat the people around them and how they treat themselves when no one else is looking.

Someone claims that God is love, yet devalues or abuses themselves or others, they do not truly believe in their heart that God is love. However, if they do believe that God is love, it will manifest very clearly by how they esteem themselves and others. It is amazing how often we are told by religion of all kinds that "God is love," yet somehow during the program, end up feeling devalued and worth very little at best.

What is the thing that all the major world religions are often telling us at our heart level? What are they telling us about our worth? They are telling us that worth is achieved, worth is earned, worth is gained. If you follow the rules of your respective religion and check all the right boxes, you can increase your sense of worth and feelings of peace and acceptance. This has placed a great burden on people. It has not relieved the troubles we already have and has added on many others. These burdens increase our feeling of not measuring up. Our problem is compounded because now we feel like we don't measure up in the eyes of others or God. In this condition, religious burnout can occur and hope can be lost. Maybe you have felt worse after attending a church service than when you first arrived; more keenly aware of all you were expected to do, not to do, and all you'd left undone. Rather than your load being lifted by grace, it was made heavier by the expectations of others. I know, it has happened to me.

The amazing thing is that those who claim to love us, and are speaking to us in His name of unconditional love, are often the ones who burn this message into our hearts. What kind of spiritual and emotional abuse is this? The great tragedy is the heartfelt way in which we come to believe that we have not managed to be worthwhile yet. Perhaps we feel if we try just a little harder to get rid of this habit, or to give even more to others, maybe one day it will all be better. It never is!

We may, however, experience a great burnout, despair, depression, or a loss of interest in "spiritual" things. We may feel that God has let us down and is never pleased. We may ultimately be drawn to those things, which promise us comfort, but in the end, leave us defiled and shamed. If this occurs long enough, we may end up with a complete loss of hope.

Despair will then set in and take over our hearts. No wonder the suicide and prescription anti-depressant rate is what it is. Does it shock anyone else that these things have come to be an accepted norm in our society? Though sad, we expect it and feel largely powerless to offer any solution!

Worth is not something that is <u>earned</u>; it is something that is bestowed as a gift!

Here we encounter a fundamental lesson that I believe all major religious systems have missed; ***Worth is not something that is earned; worth is something that is bestowed as a gift!*** We all have worth because of who we are in Christ. We are made in His image and represent Him in the world. Even though we are fallen, even though the beauty has been scarred, the vision has not been lost.

God's vision for us has never escaped Him. His plan has always been to restore us to where we were before doubts about our worth and His goodness crept into our minds. And to take us even higher, as we come to understand His infinite compassion and faithfulness to us. We need to see that we have been abused, devalued, and shamed in the name of religion and the name of "God." We need to be restored; our hearts need to be unshackled, to breathe and be free again, to be the beautiful people we were meant to be in the first place. We need to be permitted to feel the way we really do, to be able to say what is really on our minds and hearts, and to know that even when it is ugly, we are not devalued or worth less.

We are loved, and the most incredible plan is underway to get us to the place of total restoration and freedom, regardless of what our current state seems to be. The most heroic, sacrificial undertaking is now in full swing, to restore us to being the glorious kings and queens of this earth, as the real God intended for us, and to be always provided for, to be cherished, and to know our value and that of all other human beings. We may have lost that vision and defiled ourselves in the attempt to regain it, but the vision is not lost, and we are not hopeless!

What we have failed to see is our value to someone else. Do we not long to, above all things, be valuable to someone else above all other things? Is not the heart of all relational dysfunction the fact that our hearts are made to function freely only when we know that we matter more to someone else than anything else, and we have not found that to be the case? Don't we long to know that the one we love places us above everything else and will always choose us over family, friends, job, hobbies, and everything?

Recently, I heard of a husband who wrote a resignation letter and gave it to his wife to send to his boss if the job ever came between them! Now that is standing for someone and making them the priority. Sadly, this is definitely not the norm. Don't you hate when you feel that your loved one won't stand up for you? Don't you fear that God won't stand up for you, but only be truly good to you when you somehow have managed to be worthy? Isn't unbelief what caused the fall in Eden?

What caused Eve to eat the apple? Wasn't it the feeling that she wasn't worthy enough, or God good enough, to give her His very best that caused Eve to take the fruit, trying to give herself something better than she thought God was willing to give?

Isn't it what has caused the breakdown of every relationship we've ever been in? Isn't it the thing that makes us feel distant and alienated from God? If we could be convinced that we do have that place in His heart, of total and unconditional love and acceptance, regardless of our current state. Wouldn't that be a huge relief and change everything?

Wouldn't it eventually cause us to leave behind the false comforts, as we see that we are worth so much that we don't need these lesser things to drag us down from our high position? Wouldn't it relieve our minds and bring peace to our souls, just knowing that we have a worth that nothing, not even our own failings, can take away? Wouldn't it be comforting and encouraging to know that even in the midst of our darkest thinking, and the things we have done as a result, that someone values us enough to initiate the most incredible rescue campaign ever imagined?

Do you know that you are that one? Do you know that you have that worth? Do you know that the rescue has been completed? The only real question now is how to get you to see your worth as real.

Why else do our hearts love the epic films and rejoice in the strong ones who fight for and rescue the weak? We love those heroes. We want them to come for us! Don't our hearts feel a sense of peace and security when we see them on the screen and think of them? Don't you love William Wallace, willing to fight, and be tortured, and to die for freedom for his land and beloved people? Don't you love Neo, who would risk all Zion to save his beloved Trinity?

In The Lord of the Rings[1] trilogy we have a wizard

named Gandalf. He is the hero; he is the wise and strong one who loves those little Hobbits and who desires, at the risk of his own life, to fight for the salvation of Middle-earth, to see them be free and safe. Remember the scene on the bridge of Khazad Dum when Gandalf stands between the huge fiery Bal Rog and the little, frightened, weary group of his friends who are don't understand or have the strength to stand against such a foe? How our hearts cheered as he stands, recounting who he is to the Bal Rog and then demands that he return to the shadows, slams his staff on the bridge, causing it to crumble beneath the Bal Rog, and proclaims "you shall not pass!" Wow, at that point, I'm almost out of my chair in the theater!

Finally, finally, the hero has come through; he has stood his ground in the most desperate hour, and he has fought for, and safely delivered, his cherished friends against all odds! But, just after his amazing victory and the rescue of his friends, as the Bal Rog is falling, he lashes out his whip, grabs Gandalf by the ankle, and Gandalf falls into the abyss. My heart was crushed. I was in tears sitting in the theater. I couldn't believe that the one in whom I had come to feel such a sense of confidence and security could have possibly fallen.

However, all is not as it appears. Though the loss of Gandalf was almost unbearable for his fellowship, he was not lost forever. In the sequel, Gandalf reappears to them, now not as Gandalf the Grey, but as Gandalf the White. In his time lost in the depths of the earth, he transformed and returned stronger and more radiant than ever. He needed to fall and be resurrected to lead his beloved ones through what will be their most difficult hour. Later in the movie, just as Middle-earth is to face a battle of colossal proportion, as the armies of the Dark Lord are assembled against them at Helm's Deep, Gandalf tells them that he is leaving them again, but tells them to look to the east at daybreak on the morning of the fifth day.

In the battle that ensues and the incredibly poignant death of the Elf-lord Haldir and the breakthrough of their defenses, just when it seems that the enemy has overcome them, a glimmer of light appears over the eastern horizon. As they look to the east on that morning of the fifth day, Gandalf appears, gloriously mounted on a gleaming white charger, staff in hand, at the head of an enormous cavalry, which comes breaking like an ocean wave over the crest of the hill and onto the battlefield where the enemy is overthrown in a magnificent defeat.

This story is a picture of what Christ did for us. He also appears in our most desperate hour to defeat the enemy that we can't and reassure us of His unconditional love. Compare this message of love to that of old religious ideas. It was thought that your good works add to your worth and that you should keep striving to be better no matter how heartbroken and weary you are. What a bunch of rot! And the fact that it is done in God's name makes him out to be the tyrant of the universe. Who could be more insensitive, less caring, if God is how He has been portrayed to be? No wonder people who are really in touch with their needs, losses, and suffering in this life don't want to darken the door of a church, mosque, temple, shrine, etc. Our hearts are devastated enough already, who can stand another burden placed on them in the name of "God" to burden us further? Who can stand one more message telling us we must somehow improve ourselves if we are to ever measure up? Who can stand to have to hide who they really are for fear of letting some pious religious person find out about our true weaknesses, only to be condemned and rejected once more?

Remember the religious leaders of Jesus' day? What did they do when they found a woman committing adultery? They dragged her from the bed to Jesus and picked up stones to use to kill her! Sound familiar? But what was Jesus' response? They told him that the Law of Moses commanded that she be killed by stoning and asked what He would say. He bent down and began to write in the sand. As He did, they all, from the oldest to the youngest, turned and walked away. When they had left, Jesus turned to the woman and asked: "Woman where are they? Did no one condemn you?" She said, "No one, Lord,"

Let me add here that when Jesus shows up in our defense, there will be no one who will condemn us either. The only condemnation, I believe, will be for those who made Him out as our accuser and kept us from believing the truth about His heart for us, and our value to Him. Then the cavalry appears coming over the horizon at daybreak when Jesus says to her, "Neither do

I condemn you, go your way and sin no more."

Listen to these words, you whose soul hasn't had a breath of freedom from condemnation for years, who are forever living under a sense of not measuring up, who have failed in more ways than you can count, ***"neither do I condemn you!"***

This is the heart of God toward you! Now let me say, this message of freedom from condemnation must sink into our hearts (and it may take a long time for it to finally be totally believed) before we can even begin to think about doing anything right. Please note that the freedom from condemnation, the forgiveness, must occur before we can ever have a chance of not doing things wrong. The reason is this: until we know that we are safe, loved, forgiven, and secure, we will always be driven to find something to comfort us in this life, and it will drive us into the darkness looking for it. Some things may readily appear dark, others may appear to be good, but in our hearts, we are still doing them to try to meet an unmet need for love, esteem, belonging, recognition, or security. In that, even the good becomes dark for us, since it is wrong motives that drive it.

Only when our value, our worth, our place of security, and being loved, is no longer at risk, can our hearts have peace and be free from the obsession to find love, peace, or pleasure. These things leave us, and others, defiled in the attempt, adding to our sense of worthlessness and desperation, and making the addiction cycle all the more intense. As our need increases, our addictions increase. As our addictions increase, our sense of worthlessness and desire for escape increase, making our addictions increase even more. This cycle will continue until the truth of our worth, forgiveness, and the vision of our original beauty and glory is restored to us. It will happen through revelation, not our own attempts at self-improvement!

Good, kind, loving, noble, and beautiful acts are ***always the result of a heart having been restored to know its own worth and the worth of others, they are never the means to it!*** Because until a heart is truly restored to know its own worth, all its attempts at doing good, are in fact, a selfish attempt to regain a lost sense of worth. Isn't it obvious that no true good can come from one who doesn't realize they have worth, since a heart that doesn't know its own worth, can't possibly impart a sense of worth to another?

Attempting to keep religious law can never set anyone free, because what do laws do? Laws reveal that we are, by nature, lawbreakers! Seeing a speed limit sign on the highway doesn't make me one who obeys the speed limit, it only serves to reveal that I am by nature a lawbreaker, as I am usually speeding! So it is with all religious law. Laws only exist where human nature is self-seeking.

If we could see our own value and the value of others, we would need no laws to tell us to be good or considerate, because we would already be so mindful of the value of human life that we would never consider doing

Heart Issues and Religion

anything to jeopardize it in any way. When someone is striving to keep the laws in the name of religion, what they are really saying is "I know my heart isn't restored or right; therefore, I am trying so hard to do what I think I should do, even though something inside me opposes me every step of the way." Now, where does that internal opposition come from? Our hearts are not made to perform in order to be loved. *Our hearts were created to be loved. Once we realize that they are loved, all manner of good will pour out from them spontaneously!*

> **Our hearts were created to be loved. Once we realize that they are loved, all manner of good will pour out from them spontaneously!**

Until our hearts realize that they matter more than anything, nothing good will come from them. We will only strive to appear good. There will be only frustration coupled with an intense defense of the system we are hoping to find worth in, through our behavior modification program. It is amazing how valiantly a person will often fight for something they know isn't working. Why is this? It is because they have no other hope, and without their feeble and failing attempts at self-improvement, they will have no hope at all!

So how do we restore all the good we have lost in the world? By trying harder? No! We need to realize that we have always been loved and all has been sacrificed for our restoration We need to see the worth we all have to the God in whose image we are made, and Who has done all to see us made whole again, forgiven and clean. This may seem unreal to you, but let me remind you, "if a lie often told is finally believed, how much more the truth, though it seems impossible!"

Over the past number of years, I have been privileged to have several Muslim friends. Now, every time we think of ordering pizza, we have a major dilemma. Since I love all kinds of sausage products and when I think of pizza, I automatically think of Pepperoni and Italian sausage. Muslims don't eat any pork products, so we have to figure out ways to work around this. Once in a very candid conversation with one of my Muslim friends, I brought up the issue of pepperoni.

I told him that when I see the suffering, heartache, and tragedy around the world, it's hard to believe that pepperoni pizza ranked high on God's list of priorities. If it did, I couldn't imagine being happy in heaven. My friend responded with one of the best and most honest replies I have ever heard. He said that there are many terrible things we can't control, so we focus on small things we can control to make ourselves feel better. Now isn't that the heart of religion today? We have such monumental forces playing on our hearts and so many bad things that are so deeply rooted in us that we fear to even mention them, let alone hope for any real change. So we pick a ritual or something unique to make us feel like we are getting somewhere. Meanwhile, we overlook the heart issues that are causing all the real problems. We are clinging to the lie that we must perform better to be valuable and have failed to believe the truth that we are, and always have been, of greater worth than we can imagine, just because we are who we are and that God has seen fit and been pleased to make it so.

Personal note:

I was driving across a bridge and watching the rain fall when I had my first spiritual awakening. I was listening to The Who on the radio and they were singing, "Only love can bring the rain, that falls like tears from on high."[2] In that moment, I realized that there is a love on high, greater than all our experiences in this fragile, broken life. Shortly thereafter, images of Jesus that I had heard about growing up came back to me. I saw Him as the only whole person who had ever lived. I knew that all the rest of us were trying to find meaning and wholeness. I also knew that He was meaning and wholeness, even as He healed all who came to Him during His life on earth. Following this new understanding and longing for more, I became involved with the church.

This Was My Undoing—Almost

Needing to know more about Jesus, what He did for me, and His love for me, I threw myself into all sorts of activities. I was gifted, and churches always need gifted people to do things.

And things I did! For thirteen years, I did so many things. Unfortunately, there was no one who could really see my need and speak to it. Involvement and serving were highly valued. Therefore, I believed I was valued for what I did. After thirteen years, I was so exhausted, and so utterly unable to explain what I really needed, that all I could do was walk out with nothing else to give.

I felt like the worst kind of failure. In my need, I tried to numb my pain of perceived failure with drugs and alcohol, and social acceptance and popularity to find a sense of wholeness. However, instead of wholeness, this only brought dependence and chains. I couldn't fill my heart on my own and that realization created the desire for more numbness and escape, which made me feel even more like a failure. Amazingly, during this painful haze I had created, I somehow always knew that God had not given up on me.

I recall waking up on a sofa in a friend's apartment in Washington D.C. one morning, with a terrible hangover, and in that moment had the greatest sense that God was with me and that He was going to do in me what I could not do in all my best efforts.

For the next thirteen years, He began to draw me to His heart. He led me to books by others who felt burnt out on religion, and who had been restored in His faithful love. He began to work in my heart. It was a work that spoke messages of truth to my deepest areas of need, and my belief of the lies about my worth and identity.

For years I had thought I would never darken the

door of a church again. However, as my growth and understanding of how God sees me grew, I began to want to share that in a larger community. After several attempts with churches, which didn't "click", I'm happy to say that my wife and I, at the time of this publication, have found a church which is very passionate about continually growing in the knowledge of God's heart for each of us, and in sharing that message of healing and worth with others.

However, there are many churches and religious institutions that need this. Many are hurt, broken, and suffering from the messages they have received at the hands of those who neither understand nor truly believe in all God has declared us to be.

If this describes you, and my experiences resonate with you in some way, the words below were written for you:

God has not left you. God is not angry with you. God is deeply in love with you and is working tirelessly in every situation to see you restored to His heart, and wholeness in every area of your life.

Like the father of the prodigal son in Luke 15, God sees your need, is running toward you, throwing His arms around you, and kissing you. He is putting clean, gleaming robes on you that cover any dirt, giving you the family signet ring, and killing the fatted calf to throw a party that can be heard across heaven. It is said that there is great joy in the presence of the angels over one wayward person who changes their mind about God. I always heard that the angels were joyful when this happened. However, the actual verse says that there is joy in the presence of the angels. So whose joy is it? It is the joy of our Father, who made us in perfect love and who, because of Jesus' taking all our wrongs when He was crucified, can only see us perfect and whole.

Now that's a value statement I pray all will receive. After all, it is for everyone!

APPLICATION EXERCISE:

- How do you really think that God sees you and feels about you?

  - Zephaniah 3:17 says, "The Lord your God in your midst, The Mighty One, will save; He will rejoice over you with gladness, He will quiet you with His love, He will rejoice over you with singing." How does this compare to the image you have? How does this make you feel?

  - How do you think God sees you when you make a mistake, or do something wrong?

  - Hebrews 8:12 says, "For I will be merciful to their unrighteousness, and their sins and their lawless deeds I will remember no more."

  - How do you feel knowing God never remembers your wrongs and only has mercy toward you?

  - Is there anything that comes to mind that you need to be healed or forgiven for? Tell God about it and ask Him in, thanking Him for His forgiveness in Jesus and His healing of all areas. Ask Him to continually show you His love for you in your heart, by His word and His spirit.

NOTES

NOTES

ENDNOTES:

[1] Lord of the Rings, book/movie. J.R.R. Tolkien, 1954. https://en.wikipedia.org/wiki/The_Lord_of_the_Rings

[2] Love Reign O'er Me, song. Lyrics by Pete Townshend, performed by The Who, 1972. https://en.wikipedia.org/wiki/Love,_Reign_o%27er_Me

CHAPTER EIGHT:
Now and Forever—The Restoration of All Things

"Let love live, let love be, let a human heart go free. Give courage, give romance, teach them all how they can dance."[1]
—*Cirque du Soleil*

"Only love can bring the rain, that makes you yearn for the sky. Only love can bring the rain, that falls like tears from on high. Love reign o'er me, love reign o'er me."[2]
—*The Who*

All of us have received false messages about our true identity and worth, and the reality is that none of us have responded as we should by rejecting lies and believing the truth. If truth be told, we are as guilty as we are injured. Not only have we been the recipients of many false messages about our worth and value, but we have also communicated false messages to others through our words, actions, attitudes, and motives. Therefore, our restoration must involve both forgiveness of our wrongs as well as the healing of our self-worth so that we can be who we were created to be.

To see how restoration truly occurs, let us revisit the original vision of the very high place we were created to have. Through Adam and Eve" before "We fell grasp the vision of how valuable we were to God. We didn't believe that He could value us enough to give us the best. In disbelief, which is the original sin, we set out to fill our appetites with forbidden fruits of all kinds. We have defiled ourselves and others and have sinned against perfect Love.

Now perfect Love cannot throw away its beloved one because they failed and are fallen. Neither can perfect love approve or accept anything that defiles anyone. So there was a tough decision made in heaven before we ever came into existence. Actually, no decision had to be made since God's own nature dictates forever what He will do. But for the sake of our time-oriented understanding, we'll view it as a decision.

God wanted someone to share life with, so He

could either create us with the capacity for free will, understanding, love, and appreciation or create us like robots with no free will. So, He chose to make us creatures of incredible beauty, intellect, and choice. The problem was that freewill also gave us the ability to believe a lie, and to make choices that could injure ourselves, and our relationships.

However, true love never gives up, even when injured. So, God made us, loving us beyond imagination, while hating the injury we caused to ourselves, others, and Him, as a result of our unbelief in our worth and His goodness to us. He was then faced with the issue of getting rid of the unbelief and its horrible consequences and restoring us to the original vision of worth and beauty that He had in mind all along. If He let things run their natural course, our spirits, souls, and bodies would die.

> **The problem was that freewill also gave us the ability to believe a lie, and to make choices that could injure ourselves, and our relationships.**

What is the point of creating something and loving it so much, only to let it die? Perfect Love chose to do the only thing that could be done. Die in our place and suffer the consequences of all our unbelief in His goodness and love. God's own spirit came to live in a human body in the person of Jesus so that He could take the consequences of all our unbelief about our worth, and His goodness, and die in our place. There is nothing we could do to ever be worthy of this.

It is Solely Because God Sees Us as Worth That Much

It is in His nature and not a result of us trying to be good or worthy to love us that much. There was no extreme He wouldn't go to to get us back. Nothing He wouldn't do to restore us to the original vision of beauty and worth He has had for us all along. To realize we are worth the suffering of that cross, and the alienation from all that is good, beautiful, and that is God Himself, as Jesus experienced it during that eternal moment of rejection by God, while He was on the cross; is the knowledge that will forever restore our sense of worth.

Trust in God's Love and all He has accomplished, will triumph over all that has been taken away at the hands of other people. It will forever speak to us of Love that will never, ever give up on us. It brings both the forgiveness we need and the restoration to worth and value that will silence the drive to attain meaning in some way and will restore us to the Love we were made to have and give.

Here we find the true work of God and the meaning of all the suffering and heartache that has taken place in our lives. We thought we had been robbed of worth, value, and joy. But God, in His wisdom, has been taking all forces against us and intended for our destruction and has been working tirelessly to turn our situation around and work it for our good, causing us to realize the great worth that has been given to us and that no one can ever take away.

Just as his brothers sold Joseph as a slave in Egypt, so we have been sold by those who should have loved us but allowed the worst to befall us. For once the seeds of being devalued are planted in our hearts, all our choices will ultimately bring nothing but pain and destruction until the belief in our value is restored.

Just as Joseph was abandoned by his brothers, but not by God, so we too have not been abandoned by God, but are being supported, and brought to a place of honor beyond all our wildest imaginings and desires. No wonder Jesus said, "All things are possible to him who believes." Mk 9:23. This is also the reason that Paul could say, "For momentary, light affliction is producing for us an eternal weight of glory far beyond comparison ..." 2 Cor 4:17.

Throughout our lives, God has been working to replace the vision we came to have of ourselves, which was based on the devaluing we received, with His true vision of our beauty and worth. Once we believe this, God's spirit is no longer outside of us, trying to show us the new vision. His spirit is now inside us, living in us, and always confirming the vision that has been in God's heart! What He once was outside of us trying to convince us of, He is now on the inside confirming in us.

This is Referred to as Being "Born Again"

Once we receive this new perspective by faith, though we look the same outwardly, we now have a new spirit living in our hearts and showing us life from the true perspective. The lovely thing about this is once we see the truth about ourselves and others, we can never be blind to it again. As the skin horse told the Velveteen Rabbit, "once you are real, you can't become unreal again, it lasts for always."[3]

Though there may be moments when we struggle and feel the same way we used to, it is only because there is still some area where the vision hasn't been applied to the disesteem we suffered in some way. As these new issues arise, we can take great comfort in knowing that it is only because there is some new area in which God is working to set us free. We can rest assured that everything that happens will ultimately result in greater and greater vision, freedom, and appreciation of all we are and have been given. This will go on throughout this life, until the day that we see God perfectly, and as a result, become like He is forever.

This is Referred to as "Eternal Life"

May we, as King Leonidas and his valiant 300, who gave their lives to stand against the tyranny of King Xerxes and his innumerable armies[4], stand as true men and women in the war against our own souls, the souls of our families, friends, and every living person on earth. May we, as that one solitary figure, nailed to a Roman cross over 2000 years ago, look on the multitudes of those who have wronged us, and pronounce forgiveness. May we look to that One and know the forgiveness for all wrongs we have ever done in our ignorance of the worth and value we have always had to Him.

As is so often quoted at weddings, but is so seldom lived out, "(Love) bears all things, believes all things, hopes all things, endures all things. Love never fails ..." 1 Cor 13:7-8 So it is, and we, the beloved, are the recipients of such lavish love and honor. May we see the day come to pass when we know the worth we have, the worth of all others, and the grace of God, which never lost the vision of our worth, but has given His all to see us restored.

Your day is coming. This is your destiny!

APPLICATION EXERCISE:

- Take a few minutes to sit or lie very quietly. Get comfortable and still.

- Now picture a very loving mother, tenderly caring for her child. See the love in her eyes and heart, see her cleansing away and protecting the child from everything that is not good for it.

- Now see God seeing you in that way. See Him sweeping away from your heart and mind every thought about yourself that isn't perfect love. Feel His love permeating your mind, your emotions, your whole being. See Him perfectly forgiving you of all the wrongs you have done and hear Jesus on the cross say, "…It is finished…" Jn 19:30, and know your wrongs will never, ever be brought up again by God.

- Think of the incredible love for you and the value that Jesus saw in you that caused Him to suffer the terrible beatings and crucifixion because He wanted you to live abundantly, free from your past mistakes, and free forever from being devalued. See Him lifting you to the highest place, right beside Him in heaven.

- Know now that the wonders of perfect love and all the other wonders of this universe are yours as a gift. Nothing you do could ever earn this. You were chosen in the heart of God long before you were ever born. There has never been a time you weren't known and loved, and purposed to be restored, to all the good that will ever exist.

NOTES

NOTES

ENDNOTES:

[1] Let Love Live, song. Performed by Cirque du Soleil in Alegría, 1999. Produced by Canada Television and Cable Production, Cirque du Soleil Images, Egmond Film and Television, Lampo di Vita Films, Mainstream, Storia Films, Telefilms Equity Investment Program, Téléfilm Canada. https://www.imdb.com/title/tt0123376/

[2] Love Reign O'er Me, song. Lyrics by Pete Townshend, performed by The Who, 1972. https://en.wikipedia.org/wiki/Love,_Reign_o%27er_Me

[3] The Velveteen Rabbit, book. Written by Margery Williams, illustrated by William Nicholson, 1988. https://www.amazon.com/Velveteen-Rabbit-Margery-Williams/dp/0757303331/ref=tmm_hrd_swatch_0?_encoding=UTF8&qid=&sr=1

[4] 300, movie. Warner Bros., Legendary Pictures, Virtual Studios, 2006. https://www.imdb.com/title/tt0416449/

Afterward:

Thank you so much for joining me in thinking through our lives and hopefully coming to a better understanding of that real struggle that faces us all. As I trust is clear now, the real battle between good and evil lies right in the midst of our hearts, where we either agree or disagree, with the messages presented to us about our identity and value. There are so many messages that come at us through various avenues and people, which could diminish our sense of worth and value. It is how we process these messages and what we choose to believe that determines the outcome of our lives, not the things that happen themselves.

My prayer, and the reason for writing this book (which initially was written just for a friend), is that the truth of your unspeakable worth and value will be clearly seen and give you the right thoughts with which to combat any negative message about who and Whose you are. Stand firm, my friends, in the truth God declares to be true of you.

You are more than you think. You are designed in a beautiful and incredible way that no human effort could ever produce. You are here to develop and use your gifts to be a blessing to others, and in turn, to be blessed yourself. You are making an eternal difference each day, in the way you think about yourself and others, and in the ways you communicate the truth of their great worth to them in ways small and great.

The following sections include some resources to further help you on your growth journey into all you were created to be.

"He has brought me to His banquet hall, and His banner over me is love."

—Song of Solomon 2:4

"You prepare a table (of bread and wine, symbolic of the body and blood of Jesus, given for you) before me in the presence of my enemies (every accuser, every lie about your worth); You have anointed my head with oil, my cup overflows."

—Psalm 23:5

APPENDIX 1:
Who I Am—In Christ!

(Originally compiled by Neil Anderson)

Our feelings can be tricky things, and easily led into making agreements with the past ways we have felt about ourselves, God, others, and life.

We must always call them up short by reminding ourselves of the truth.

A good way to do that is to take time to reflect on what we were feeling/are feeling, in a given situation. Once we identify the thought behind the feeling, we can replace it with the truth God declares to be true of us, in Christ.

The following list is a great place to start. I like to write a few of these down each morning, before I have to do anything, say them out loud several times, and picture this reality in my mind and heart. I often end up bowed before such love and truth, the Truth that for many, many years I did not know or believe.

WHO I AM—IN CHRIST

(Originally complied by Neil Anderson)

I AM ACCEPTED...

John 1:12 I am God's child

John 15:15 As a disciple (learner), I am a friend of Jesus Christ.

Romans 5:1 I have been justified (declared righteous)

1 Corinthians 6:17 I am united with the Lord, and am one with Him in Spirit.

1 Corinthians 6:19-20 I have been bought with a price and I belong to God.

1 Corinthians 12:27 I am a member of Christ's body

Ephesians 1:3-8 I have been chosen by God and adopted as His child.

Colossians 1:13-14 I have been redeemed and forgiven of all my sins.

Colossians 2:9-10 I am complete in Christ.

Hebrews 4:14-16 I have direct access to the throne of grace through Jesus Christ.

I AM SECURE...

Romans 8:1-2 I am free from condemnation (since Jesus took it all).

Romans 8:28 I am assured that God works for my good in all circumstances.

Romans 8:31-39 I am free from any condemnation brought against me and I cannot be separated from the love of God.

2 Corinthians 1:21-22 I have been established, anointed and sealed by God.

Colossians 3:1-4 I am hidden with Christ in God.

Philippians 1:6 I am confident that God will complete the good work He began in me.

Philippians 3:20 I am a citizen of heaven.

2 Timothy 1:7 I have not been given a spirit of fear but of power, love, and a sound mind.

1 John 5:18 I am born of God and the evil one cannot touch me.

I AM SIGNIFICANT...

John 15:5   I am a branch of Jesus Christ, the true vine, and a channel of His life.

John 15:16   I have been chosen and appointed to bear fruit.

1 Corinthians 3:16   I am God's temple.

2 Corinthians 5:17-21   I am a minister of reconciliation for God.

Ephesians 2:6   I am seated with Jesus Christ in the heavenly realm.

Ephesians 2:10   I am God's workmanship (and God doesn't make junk!)

Ephesians 3:12   I may approach God with freedom and confidence.

Philippians 4:13   I can do all things through Christ, Who strengthens me.

Appendix 1: Who I Am—In Christ!

The following columns, on the next several pages, are for you to write down the beliefs and feelings that trouble you.

Then you can claim the truth that is the opposite of the lie about your value and worth contained in the feeling.

There is a cute poem I heard many years ago that sums up the connection between feeling, faith, and fact very nicely:

"Three men walked upon a wall, Feeling, Faith, and Fact. Feeling took an awful fall, and Faith was taken back.

Faith was so close to Feeling that he fell too. But Fact remained and pulled Faith up, and that brought Feeling too."

FEELING & BELIEFS	TRUTHS OF GOD

Appendix 1: Who I Am—In Christ!

FEELING & BELIEFS	TRUTHS OF GOD

FEELING & BELIEFS	TRUTHS OF GOD

Appendix 1: Who I Am—In Christ!

FEELING & BELIEFS	TRUTHS OF GOD

FEELING & BELIEFS	TRUTHS OF GOD

Appendix 2:
A Note On Forgiveness

In response to all the messages we have looked at in this book, it is important to realize that for every instance in which we have received a negative message or action from another, that forgiveness is needed. With this in mind, I'd like to list a few thoughts about what forgiveness is and isn't:

1. Forgiveness isn't saying that what happened was OK in any way.

2. Forgiveness is realizing that the messages conveyed about our identity and worth by others, through their words and actions, were false and our offenders could not see clearly to understand our true value.

3. Forgiveness is letting go of all the desire for retribution. This is somewhat easier once we realize that the thinking and actions of the ones who

hurt us, are characteristic of their lives and are creating for them a terrible series of consequences already. God has said "Vengeance is Mine, I will repay." Giving them to God to deal with and releasing them on our end, sets us free. We can even desire that they come to their senses and understand their own worth and that of others (which is what God wants and what Jesus died for). Often it is those who were abused in some way, who devalue and abuse others. Healing for all is the goal here.

4. Forgiveness isn't forgetting. Forgiveness is stepping down from the judgment throne and pronouncing, "I do not pass judgment on you any longer". "You are God's, He will set things right, for my part I pronounce blessing on you."

   You may never forget what happened, but you don't need to. Each time you remember, step down from judgment and hand them over to God. He will judge rightly!

You may never forget what happened, but you don't need to. Each time you remember, step down from judgment and hand them over to God. He will judge rightly!

A recent Facebook post said, "If we don't heal what hurt us, we'll bleed on those who didn't cut us." May we all be healed and seek the healing of all, that we can be in a place to bless others, not wound them.

REFERENCES:
Aggregated Endnotes

Chapter One

[1] Babe, movie. Universal pictures; Kennedy Miller Productions, 1995, https://www.imdb.com/title/tt0112431/companycredits?ref=ttdtco

[2] Calvin and Hobbes, Bill Watterson. Andrews McMeel Publishing, 1985-1995, https://en.wikipedia.org/wiki/Calvin_and_Hobbes

Chapter Two

[1] Why Does My Heart Feel So Bad? Written and performed by Moby, 1999. Label- Mute, https://www.amazon.com/Why-Does-Heart-Feel-Bad/dp/B00002ZZNI

Chapter Three

¹ Forrest Gump, movie. Paramount Pictures (presents) (A Steve Tisch/Wendy Finerman Production by) (A Robert Zemeckis Film), 1994. https://www.imdb.com/title/tt0109830/

² Footprints in the Sand, poem. Mary Fishback Powers. https://www.onlythebible.com/Poems/Footprints-in-the-Sand-Poem.html

Chapter Four

¹ Subdivisions, song. Lyrics Neal Peart, performed by Rush, 1982. https://www.imdb.com/title/tt5859724/

² Calvin and Hobbes, Bill Watterson. Andrews McMeel Publishing, 1985-1995. https://en.wikipedia.org/wiki/Calvin_and_Hobbes

³ Molder of Dreams, book. Guy Doud. Focus on the Family, 1990. https://www.amazon.com/Molder-Dreams-Guy-Rice-Doud/dp/1561790273/ref=s-r_1_1?keywords=molder+of+dreams&qid=1556122143&s=gateway&sr=8-1

⁴ Cider House Rules, movie. Film Colony, Miramax, Nina Saxon Film Design, 1999. https://www.imdb.com/title/tt0124315/

⁵ Seinfeld, miniseries. West Shapiro, Castle Rock

Entertainment, 1989-1998. https://www.imdb.com/title/tt0098904/companycredits?ref=ttdtco

⁶ John Maxwell, author, speaker. https://en.wikipedia.org/wiki/John_C._Maxwell, www.johnmaxwell.com

Chapter Five

¹ Rockstar, song. Nickelback, 2005, https://www.amazon.com/Rockstar-Explicit/dp/B0011Z0YR2/ref=sr11?keywords=rockstar+nickelback&qid=1556122828&s=gateway&sr=8-1

² Middletown Dreams, song. Lyrics by Neal Peart, performed by Rush, 1985. https://www.rush.com/songs/middletown-dreams/

³ 9 to 5, song. Dolly Parton, 1980. https://www.azlyrics.com/lyrics/dollyparton/9to5.html

⁴ Joe vs the Volcano, movie. Warner Brothers, Amblin Entertainment, 1990. https://www.imdb.com/title/tt0099892/

⁵ No Little People, book. Francis Shaeffer, 2003. https://www.amazon.com/Little-People-Introduction-Udo-Middelmann-ebook/dp/B0026IUO82/ref=sr_1_fkmrnull_1?crid=3TKMEAD95TOSA&keywords=no+little+people+schaeffer&qid=1556125013&s=gateway&sprefix=no+little+people%2Caps%2C221&sr=8-1-fkmrnull

Chapter Six

¹ Harden My Heart, song. Written by Marv Ross, performed by Quarterflash, 1981. https://en.wikipedia.org/wiki/Harden_My_Heart

² Emotion Detector, song. Lyrics by Neal Peart, performed by Rush, 1985. https://www.rush.com/songs/emotion-detector/

³ Wizard of Oz, movie. Metro-Goldwyn-Mayer, 1939. https://www.imdb.com/title/tt0032138/

⁴ The Matrix Reloaded, movie. Warner Bros., Village Roadshow Pictures, Silver Pictures, NPV Entertainment, Heineken Branded Entertainment, 2003.

Chapter Seven

¹ Lord of the Rings, book/movie. J.R.R. Tolkien, 1954. https://en.wikipedia.org/wiki/The_Lord_of_the_Rings

² Love Reign O'er Me, song. Lyrics by Pete Townshend, performed by The Who, 1972. https://en.wikipedia.org/wiki/Love,_Reign_o%27er_Me

Chapter Eight

¹ Let Love Live, song. Performed by Cirque du Soleil in Alegría, 1999. Produced by Canada Television and Cable Production, Cirque du Soleil Images,

References

Egmond Film and Television, Lampo di Vita Films, Mainstream, Storia Films, Telefilms Equity Investment Program, Téléfilm Canada. https://www.imdb.com/title/tt0123376/

[2] Love Reign O'er Me, song. Lyrics by Pete Townshend, performed by The Who, 1972. https://en.wikipedia.org/wiki/Love,_Reign_o%27er_Me

[3] The Velveteen Rabbit, book. Written by Margery Williams, illustrated by William Nicholson, 1988. https://www.amazon.com/Velveteen-Rabbit-Margery-Williams/dp/0757303331/ref=tmm_hrd_swatch_0?_encoding=UTF8&qid=&sr=1

[4] 300, movie. Warner Bros., Legendary Pictures, Virtual Studios, 2006. https://www.imdb.com/title/tt0416449/

Biography:

Jeff Byrd is a native and resident of Norfolk, Virginia. He is the owner of Jeffrey Byrd Coaching and a certified speaker, trainer, and coach with the John Maxwell Team. His purpose in life and in business is to aid others in seeing their true value, the value of others, and recognizing the gifts and abilities they've been given, in order to develop and use them to lift themselves and others to their most fulfilling life.

Jeff's passion for helping others see their own value comes from years of wrestling with a sense of personal worth. Jeff often teaches that "We can tell how valuable anything is to anyone by what they will give up for it." It wasn't until after many years of struggle that Jeff came to understand his own value to God He began to believe what God was willing to give up for him by giving Jesus for him. With this as the complete example of what servant-leadership truly is, as well as the ultimate statement of the value of every person, Jeff seeks to help individuals first realize their own worth. Then they can begin to see the worth of those around them, in their families, communities, places of work, and other organizations. This equips individuals to achieve maximum effectiveness in all they do by seeing the true value of others and developing and using their unique strengths and abilities to serve them.

Jeff hosts a weekly podcast called Empowered Living with Jeff Byrd. The podcast provides teaching and interviews, designed to up-level thinking and living in all areas of life, professional and personal. The podcast airs on iTunes, iHeart Radio, Google Play, Spotify, Spreaker, Talk Network Radio, and other stations.

Jeff also is the founder of the Byrd Young Leaders School in Pakistan. The school was founded to provide at-risk children who are generational slaves of the brick kiln industry the opportunity to learn English and other subjects. This gives them a chance to compete in the global marketplace and escape a life of making bricks by hand, all day, for one dollar per day.

Jeff sat on the board of the Endependence Center Inc. in Norfolk, VA, for 13 years. The Endependence Center is an advocacy group for those with disabilities.

He is a past president of the Virginia Beach Task Force on Aging, a former Young Life team leader, Sunday School teacher, and owner of Byrd's Eye Photography.

Jeff and his wife Angela Byrd, who is an artist and art instructor, enjoy gardening, birding, travel, the symphony, art exhibitions, wineries, and the enjoyment of good friends!

Wilson Law—Book Sponsor

- *Legacy Preservation*
- *Trust Administration*
- *Asset Protection*
- *Estate Planning*
- *Probate*
- *Elder Law*
- *Business Planning*
- *Succession Planning*

Following The Road To Peace Of Mind

FOUR LOCATIONS TO SERVE YOU

Corporate Office: 430 McLaws Circle, Suite 102 Williamsburg, VA 23185 | **Call:** 866-603-5976
Email: info@wilsonlawplc.com

By Appointment Only

11815 Fountain Way, Suite 300
Newport News, VA 23606

1 Columbus Center, Suite 600
Virginia Beach, VA 23462

8201 Greensboro Drive, Suite 300
McLean, VA 22102

Jeffrey Byrd Coaching

Vision • Direction • Fullfillment

- *Keynote Speaking*
- *Coaching*
- *Individual & Group Training*
- *Radio & Video Presenter*
- *John Maxwell Team Certified*
- *Founder and Mentor of Byrd Young Leaders School in Pakistan*

CONTACT INFORMATION TO SERVE YOU

Corporate Office:
Norfolk, Virginia

Website: www.JeffByrdCoaching.com

Email: Jeff@JeffByrdCoaching.com

By Appointment Only

Angela Byrd Designs

CREATE! Classes

- Family Gatherings
- Birthday Parties
- Date Nights
- Fundraising
- Team Building
- Art Therapy
- Art Meditation
- and More!

Create a Custom Event at Your Location or check out the Website Events Calendar & Join a Scheduled Class
www.AngelaByrdDesigns.com

Connect with us now to Schedule Your *CREATE! Classes* or to Discuss Custom Art

CONTACT INFORMATION TO SERVE YOU

Studio:
Norfolk, Virginia

Website: www.AngelaByrdDesigns.com

Email: Angela@AngelaByrdDesigns.com

By Appointment Only

Publishing with New Dominion Press

How Do I Get Started? Can I Really Get Published? Why New Dominion Press?

CONTACT INFORMATION TO SERVE YOU

Studio:
1217 Godfrey Avenue, Norfolk, Virginia 23504

Website: www.NewDominionPress.com

Email: CCChristie@NewDominionMedia.com

By Appointment Only

www.ingramcontent.com/pod-product-compliance
Lightning Source LLC
Chambersburg PA
CBHW071453080526
44587CB00014B/2097